I0022873

Adland's
Progressive
Gaze

Also by the author:

How to do better creative work;
Pearson Education Limited, 2009

Changing the world is the only fit work for a grown man;
Adworld Press, 2012

How to write better copy;
Macmillan/Bluebird Books, 2016

Um conto de duas cidades (A tale of two cities);
Blue Book, 2019

Can't sell, won't sell:
Advertising, politics and culture wars;
Adworld Press, 2020-21

The Howard Gossage Show;
Adworld Press, 2024

Adland's Progressive Gaze

How the UK advertising industry
lost sight of the people and things
that matter most

ADWORLD PRESS

Copyright © 2025 Steve Harrison
All rights reserved. No part of this publication may be
reproduced or transmitted in any form or by any means,
electronic or mechanical including photocopying, recording or
any information storage or retrieval system, without prior
permission in writing from the publishers.

The right of Steve Harrison to be identified as the author of this
work has been asserted by him in accordance with the Copyright,
Designs and Patents Act 1988.
First published in the United Kingdom in November 2025 by
Adworld Press. Cover art and text designed by Dave Dye.
Typography and layout by Rachel Woodman and Richard Powell.

ISBN 978-0-9571515-4-3

Steve Harrison

Steve Harrison was the European Exec. Creative Director (OgilvyOne) and the Worldwide Creative Director (Wunderman) either side of running his own agency, HTW, where he won more Cannes Lions in his discipline (18) than any creative director in the world. His work subsequently featured in the *D&AD Copy Book*. He has authored several books including *How to write better copy* and *How to do better creative work* - the latter being the most expensive advertising book ever when it traded on amazon at £3,854 a copy. Five years ago, he wrote *Can't Sell, Won't Sell* which was the industry's first major critique of adland's fixation with social purpose. The IPA described it as the "most provocative book in years." As Steve says, "wait 'til they see this one."

For my inspirational Mum, Olive
And Morag, who helped me work this all out

Acknowledgements

"No one's allowed to smoke,
Or tell a dirty joke,
And whistling is forbidden.

"If chewing gum is chewed,
The chewer is pursued,
And in the hoosegow hidden.

"I'll put my foot down, so shall it be.
This is the land of the free."

Rufus T. Firefly
Duck Soup (1933)

It is customary to use this part of the book to acknowledge those who've contributed to its creation. And to thank them personally with a roll call of names.

But in this case, I cannot because so many of the individuals I've spoken to have asked to remain anonymous. They are too afraid of the consequences of sharing their experiences of and opinions about life in today's advertising industry.

I am talking here about everyone from juniors to those at the very top of their profession: CEOs, CSOs and ECDs. And about black, white, brown, female, male and gay people. All of them are aware that publicly sharing a point of view that challenges, critiques or contradicts the dominant groupthink can damage their career.

Such is the climate of fear that, in our correspondence, several have chosen to use their personal emails rather than their company accounts for fear of others tracking our conversation.

And this in an industry that trumpets its commitment to always "doing the right thing", upholding "the moral imperative" and bowing to no one in its devotion to diversity and inclusion.

If this was a Marx Brothers movie such a paradox might be absurdly funny.

Unfortunately it's not - and, as you're about to see, funny is the last word you'd apply to life in adland today.

"Very well argued and fascinating to read. Gonna piss off a lot of very self-important people. But for my money, that's the only proper reason for writing a book. Congrats!"
Bob Hoffman, The Ad Contrarian

"Brisk, brutal and brilliant, *Adland's Progressive Gaze* is an invaluable history of the recent past, documenting events that many would rather forget or pretend never happened. It comes from one of adland's great copywriters, who is immersed in the tradition of seeing the buying public's point of view, and brings an instinctive respect for the 'barbarians' outside adland's gates.

"Some readers will find it an uncomfortable immersion in an alternative world view. If so, imagine being immersed in such a world view not for a single book, but for years on end, coming from every trade magazine, conference stage, awards show and LinkedIn post. This is the stifling context from which this book emerges, as a challenge and a counterpoint. Read it and reckon with it."
Nick Asbury, Author of *The Road to Hell: How Purposeful Business Leads to Bad Marketing and a Worse World. And How Human Creativity is the Way Out*

"As everyone knows, advertising is in a terrible state. In order to fix it, we need to know what went wrong. This book is a very thorough analysis of how we got into the mess we're in. If we read it, and learn from it, maybe we can begin to fix it."
Dave Trott, Creative Director, Consultant, Author

"This book is a fabulous attack on the insanely worthy and self-regarding trend in advertising where, perhaps in symbolic atonement for its past sins, it began to ask its audience to save the world every time they went shopping. The result was a decade of advertising where every ad resembled an ad for the 2008 Obama campaign with a random client logo shoehorned into the corner."
Rory Sutherland, President Emeritus, Ogilvy Consulting

"Steve's book is like a fire alarm going off in an agency - bracing, impossible to ignore and exactly what the room needs."
Marc Lewis, Dean, School of Communication Arts

Contents

1
Vibe shift

"Oh fuck, Jaguar, what have you done?"

Thus spake *Marketing Week* columnist Mark Ritson after seeing the ad that launched the rebrand of Jaguar on November 18th, 2024.[1]

The film featured a series of actors of largely indeterminate gender dressed like something from a spoof New Romantics pop video from the early 1980s.

They swung sledgehammers, swiped the screen with paint brush strokes and struck poses while captions exhorted us to: "create exuberant'", "live vivid", "delete ordinary", "break moulds" and "copy nothing".[2]

No cars were featured and, to coincide with the film's appearance, all archives on Jag's social media channels were deleted.

Gone, too, was "The Leaper" - the hood ornament previously described on the Jaguar Forums website, (aka "the world's largest international Jaguar community for news, rumors and discussion") as "a sexy, powerful image and the very definition of iconic."[3]

"Everything woke turns to shit"

Many contributors to that site echoed Mark Ritson's view. One, "vincent 661983", felt "a mixture of disappointment, betrayal, anger" and concluded "everything woke turns to shit".[4]

The New York Post seemed to agree with "vincent 661983", describing the film as "the latest example of idiotic and woke corporate virtue signalling".[5]

On the BBC's *Top Gear* website, Ollie Kew observed: "The YouTube video has had over two million views. The Instagram reel has been seen 6.9 million times and the commenter sentiment across all social media channels is overwhelmingly negative." As he observed: "The word 'woke' (and 'go woke, go broke') has been bandied about just as much as the phrase 'RIP Jaguar.'"[6]

The response from the advertising and marketing community as expressed on LinkedIn was equally damning. The strategist John James gave his thumbs down and then asked for others' opinions - offering a prize for the one that received the most likes.

The ultimate winner asked: "Is it a parody of an industry that's disappeared up its own arse?"

Amongst the 663 other replies were: "All that's missing is Sam Smith in a gimp suit on the end frame" and "This is a woefully misguided attempt to turn a British icon into a symbol of automotive wokery."[7]

Jaguar needed a re-boot

To be fair there were some who pointed out that Jaguar needed to re-boot the brand. In the last financial year, the parent company Jaguar Land Rover sold 58,000 Range Rovers, 28,700 Defenders, and just 13,528 Jaguars. And that bad performance hadn't been an aberration.

But as Mark Ritson pointed out, Jaguar needed a refresh not a rebrand. And certainly not one that made him "Laugh out loud. Not from joy or appreciation for the boldness of the new vision. But from the sheer fucking lunacy of the whole thing."[8]

Then again, others felt the "sheer lunacy" had attracted the kind of attention that had not been forthcoming for years, and applauded the chutzpah needed to be willing to court controversy. Time may prove that view to be correct. But I doubt it because it's hard to discern a business objective in all the posturing.

As this comment on LinkedIn put it: "This is coming straight out of a creative director who's 'slumming it' in advertising and absolutely in love with their own vision. Research (or even reading the room) be damned."[9]

The more you get to know the creative team's intentions, the more you realise exactly what that "vision" was.

"A diverse, inclusive and unified culture"

It came across clearly in the 30 second Instagram post featuring Jaguar's head of brand strategy, Santino Pietrosanti, that accompanied the launch. That was explicit enough. But you get the full picture from the speech from which that clip was taken.

Speaking at the Virgin Atlantic Attitude Awards for "Queer Cultural Icons", he took to the stage and explained to an excitable audience: "At Jaguar we are passionate about our people and are committed to fostering a diverse, inclusive and unified culture that is representative of not only the people who use our products but in the society in which we all live; a culture where our employees can bring their authentic selves to work, and we're on a transformative journey of our own, driven by a belief in diversity, inclusion, creativity, policy and most importantly, action. We've established over 15 DEI groups such as Pride, who are here tonight, Women in Engineering and Neuro-diversity Matters. We've launched major policy revisions such as Transitioning at Work to drive equity and support for our communities, embracing individuality as our Superpower...

... In a couple of weeks time you will see an all-new Jaguar turn up like never before. And we aren't just talking about cars, we're talking about all-new ways of thinking and embracing the full spectrum of human potential and creativity because Jaguar has always stood for fearless originality, striving to be a copy of nothing and we believe that every person has the potential to be something unique, something original and that's what makes us strong and we why we at Jaguar proudly stand with the LGBTQ+ community because we know that originality thrives in spaces where people are free to be themselves. And I can tell you, as a young gay man, I dreamed of working at a car company - as cheesy as that sounds - but I never imagined a day when I would actually have a seat at the table or the ability to realise my own dreams because it felt so far out of reach because I was terrified of being just myself. And now I'm finally here. And so together we will keep pushing forward because as long as we keep fighting, keep dreaming and keep being unapologetically ourselves, then there will always be hope."[10]

The real creative objective

It was a classic woke performance. One that was long on emotion and self-revelation But, if you stick with Santino to the end of his journey, you're left with a good idea of the creative rationale for the launch film - and its objective.

It had nothing to do with "the people who use our products" or selling cars to them. Indeed, if the car had any role in this, it was as a vehicle for the creative team's progressive point of view. And their narrow focus on a small segment of the LGBTQ+ community.

In short, Santino and his like-minded colleagues were using their privileged access to the public, and Jaguar Land Rover's sizeable marketing budget, to draw attention to the aspect of identity politics that most interests them.

In the aftermath of the negative response, JLR's chief creative officer Gerry McGovern backed his team and quipped, they "have not been sniffing the white stuff".[11]

Maybe not. But it seemed they had been swigging the Kool-Aid favoured by most of adland's major agencies and institutions throughout the previous decade. The one which, once imbibed, gave the hallucinatory impression that issues such as diversity and inclusion, the climate crisis and the pursuit of social justice must take precedence over the need to create demand, build brands and sell things.[12]

"You have completely misread the moment"

The Jag backlash indicated that this brew had gone flat. And that the marketing and advertising industry - and society in general - had had quite enough of the uninhibited progressive proselytising it had unleashed on the world.

This was certainly columnist John Gabriel's take on things when, on November 19th, he tweeted: "This is so the wrong timing for this. I can understand the

C-suite being conned into this in 2022, but you have completely misread the moment. Bud Light 2.0." [13]

As Gabriel suggested, the response to Jaguar had its precursor in the reaction to Bud Light's decision to hire trans actor/comedian Dylan Mulvaney to promote the brand.

The chief marketing officer, Alissa Heinerscheid, was responsible not only for involving Mulvaney but for the ensuing furore.

Mulvaney was not the new face of Bud Light but just one of a number of influencers who'd been asked to big up the brand. And their involvement would have gone largely unnoticed had not Heinerscheid gone public with her rationale.

Having scorned the existing "fratty" customer and their "out of touch humour" she explained "I have a really clear job to do when I took over Bud Lite to evolve and elevate ... it means inclusivity, it means shifting the tone. It means having a campaign that is truly inclusive and feels lighter and brighter. Representation is at the heart of evolution."

Have a look at the YouTube film posted on 7th September, 2023 by Martin Decoder. You'll see the same self-centred zealotry that characterised Santino Pietrosanti's approach to his job.[14]

Opening up the Overton Window

After that, those who weren't entirely happy with the way Alissa was "evolving and elevating" their favourite beer also had their say. And her decision to bring her politics to the brand resulted in a boycott which saw year-on-year sales plummet by 27% and Bud Light relinquishing its 20 year spot as the number 1 beer in the US.[15]

Clearly something was going on here. There've been bad ads in the past and ill-conceived tie-ins with famous people - remember Kendall Jenner and Pepsi? But the response to Bud Light and then Jaguar was something different. It marked a radical rejection of political correctness, and a new willingness to challenge the dominant progressive groupthink that had imposed it.

What we were seeing was the reframing of what political scientists call The Overton Window - i.e. which subjects and opinions are deemed acceptable for comment and debate, and those that remain off limits.

The outpouring of anger signalled that social purpose was well and truly up for discussion and, that most damning of criticism, ridicule.

Vibe shift

A few years earlier, when purpose reigned, this would've been called "a pivot". (Remember when everyone was "pivoting at the speed of culture"?)

Today it's a "vibe shift" - a term coined back in 2021 by Sean Monahan the trend forecasting creator of the *8Ball* newsletter.

He traced the "shift" back to the restrictions that came with Covid. "Young people who both felt like they couldn't say what they thought, but couldn't really do what they wanted to, because they were going to college through Zoom and it was illegal to go to parties in many places. These things kind of all came together with a general sense that the past was a freer, more hedonistic era."[16]

Writing in the *Financial Times,* Jemima Kelly said that, as a result, "it's no longer hip or cutting edge to be 'woke' or even proclaim that you are. Creative young people want to be countercultural and being 'woke' feels mainstream and virtually middle-aged these days."[17]

When the tremors reverberated through adland, what previously had gone unsaid for fear of censure was suddenly being openly and loudly shared and shouted.

Hence the explosion of vitriol that greeted the Jaguar launch.

We lost our collective marbles

Within adland's inner circle, the *volte-face* was best articulated by Sarah Carter, the global planning head of Adam & EveDDB. She was more incredulous than incandescent when, on January 8, 2025, she was interviewed by Jon Evans for his podcast, "The Uncensored CMO".

"That whole collective losing of our marbles over the purpose period. It would be quite good to have a COVID-like purpose Inquiry. So why exactly did we do that? Because we should learn from it.

"To me it's just a function of a lack of market orientation. We've just got to get comfortable with our insignificance in peoples' lives and that, you know, we influence the least important decisions that people make. And the best thing we can hope is that they chuck our brand in their basket without thinking about it. And that's fine.

"But instead we want other people to think what we think about life. And we want them to feel that what might be important is important. It's terrifying really when you think about what that whole period did in terms of waste of money and the implication of waste of profit."

Admirable sentiments. And she was right. There had been a scandalous and maybe even fraudulent misappropriation of clients' money by those who wanted to use those budgets to advance their own progressive point of view. And to make, as Sarah said, "other people think what we think about life."[18]

Sarah is one of the most respected thinkers in the business. And the great pity is she did not speak out sooner. But an even greater tragedy for the industry is that equally respected and clever people were active and voluble advocates of the social purpose movement that Sarah so scathingly critiqued.

Why did so few people speak out?

The simple answer is, they were afraid to. Social purpose was so entrenched in, and enforced by, adland's groupthink that only those with nothing to lose were willing to question it.

By nothing to lose, I mean they did not have a job at one of London's large agencies or one of adland's institutions. Or a HR person monitoring their thoughts and comments and possibly inviting them in for a chat to discuss the "appropriateness" of their views.

The only individuals who regularly broke ranks were Nick Asbury - a freelance writer; Andrew Tenzer and Ian Murray - who worked for Reach Solutions, the research arm of the Mirror Group of newspapers; Paul Burke - another freelance writer and Chris Bullick and Giles Edwards - who have their own independent shops - Pull and Gasp - both of which are based beyond the capital.

Otherwise, any criticism of social purpose was non-existent. Moreover, for the ten years from 2012 onwards I cannot recall a staff journalist at *The Drum* or *Campaign* championing commercial purpose over its social counterpart. Likewise there was silence on this issue from the major players at such institutions as the Advertising Association (AA), the Institute of Practitioners in Advertising (IPA), Design & Art Direction (D&AD), Women in Advertising and Communications Leadership (WACL) and the Data and Marketing Association (DMA). The same is true of the leaders of our big network agencies and the holding companies that own them.

This reluctance to speak out percolated through the ranks.

From 2020 onwards I regularly posted on LinkedIn with opinions at variance with the consensus. I could see from my dashboard that I was getting lots of views from employees of such agencies as VCCP, Adam & Eve/DDB, M&C Saatchi, Ogilvy, Dentsu, Wunderman, Accenture Song and VML. But, over a four year period, I could count on one hand the number of likes or comments from any of London's big shops.

Indeed, back then, few people stuck their head above the parapet to question the conventional view that "the answer's social purpose, now remind me again, what's the problem?"

But as the response to the Jaguar rebrand suggested, it was suddenly perfectly safe to climb atop the parapet and gesticulate rudely at the retreating ranks of purpose advocates.

Progressives still had the power

The backlash seemed robust enough. But reading through the screeds of criticism it struck me that the response was almost as OTT as the film itself.

Certainly, the critics were expressing, at volume, opinions that had been suppressed for years. And yes, they were exacting a certain revenge on those who'd been doing the suppressing.

But it struck me that there was more to it than that. I'd suggest that the violent Jag backlash gave vent to frustrations that many people still didn't feel free to articulate in their workplace.

The progressive hold over their working lives was still suffocating. Yes, social purpose had fallen from grace. But the activists' and careerists' faith remained strong. As did their grip on the levers of power in our institutions. They'd spent over a decade indoctrinating the industry and, as a result, purpose and their politicised point of view had, for many, become the default setting.

Nowhere was this more apparent than in the way the internal affairs of agency life were managed. Here the activist guardians of progressive orthodoxy had dug themselves in at HR and more specifically at the department of Diversity, Equity + Inclusion.

We'll look at how, in many ways, that's become the department of Division, Enmity and Intrusion in Part 2 of the book. And we'll see how the fixation with the current interpretation of DE+I is actually blocking the cognitive diversity adland needs. Indeed, we'll ask if it is actually diverting the industry away from addressing the much bigger existential problem that it now faces.

But in order to understand those scenarios, let's first explore how and why progressive ideology came to dominate advertising's output and institutions.

And how an industry that was renowned for its mavericks and misfits, its commitment to freethinking and disruption could succumb so supinely to this groupthink.

2
Why adland embraced social purpose

Our story goes back 30 years to that golden age when the ads were sometimes more entertaining than the programmes they interrupted. It was an era when people would sing their jingles, quote their dialogue and incorporate their taglines into everyday speech.

I remember, for example, the first time I took serious drugs and the chap who gave them to me saying, "You'll be going up that hill as fast as you come down it." Which was an observation lifted word-for-word from Ridley Scott's brilliant "Boy on a Bike" ad for Hovis bread.

Admittedly that was from the mid-'seventies. But as recently as thirty or even twenty years ago you had: "You've been Tangoed", "Happiness is a Cigar Called Hamlet", Guinness's "Surfer", BT's "It's Good to Talk", Rowan Atkinson's "Richard Latham" for Barclaycard, Sony's "Balls", Honda's "Grrr" or "Cog", Levis's "Creek", Or pretty much anything from Lynx (sorry those easily offended) or more recently, Specsavers.

There was a dynamic group of brilliant agencies - think of AMV, Mother, HHCL, BMP, TBWA, Fallon, Leagas Delaney, BBH - who had their own distinct and meticulous approaches to creating their work. These were usually time-consuming and labour-intensive.

But clients were willing to wait while the process was complete and pay for the hours - and expertise.

Why? Because the good stuff got results. The Institute of Practitioners in Advertising reckon that award winning work from these halcyon days was more effective than non-award winning ads by a factor of 12:1.[1]

In sticking to their processes and their principles, these great agencies did the rest of the industry a huge service. Not only did they elevate the business of advertising and make it culturally important. They also provided air cover to other agencies (like mine, for example) who aspired to produce entertaining, effective, ideas-driven work.

But then it all started to go horribly wrong

First came the hiving off of media planning and buying as a separate entity. This was great for those new agencies because they could roll out the metrics to prove their expertise and justify their fees.

But, as Richard Huntington, the former chief strategy officer and chairman of Saatchi & Saatchi has pointed out, the shops they left behind made the mistake of defining themselves as "Creative Agencies" and "unwittingly positioned themselves as purveyors of a commodity product".[2]

It was a decision which proved disastrous with the coming of digital.

Suddenly it was possible to create an ad in the morning and stick it in front of your prospect that afternoon. With the added promise that you could target that ad precisely at the person most likely to buy. And then, even better, strike up an interactive dialogue with them about what they might want to buy next.

The days of pushing a message were over

To be honest, it wasn't the digital creative that did the damage. It was the digital pundit. And the first blow was landed back in 1999 by a chap called Seth Godin. His *Permission Marketing* was an all out attack on what he called "interruption marketing" or all the traditional stuff like "You've been Tangoed", "Guinness Surfer" and Sony's "Balls" mentioned above.[3]

If Godin undermined the foundation upon which competitive persuasion had been built then another book, and the numerous press articles, conferences, seminars and blogs that it spawned, was even more damaging: Rick Levine's *The Cluetrain Manifesto*.[4]

Like Godin, Levine told us that the days of pushing a message out were over. We were entering a totally different era in which a technologically empowered customer pulled only those messages they wanted to receive and engaged only with those brands that they'd allow into their lives.

Not only that but, with the wonders of open source software, customers could join with the brand to create the advertising and be key players in new product development.

Suddenly those Creative Agencies seemed old fashioned, slow and expensive. And they did very little to counter that view or fight their corner.

When clients started to want the creative work quicker and cheaper, the agencies complied. And the practices and processes that had worked so well in their golden age were parked - for good.

Here come the charlatans and halfwits

Malcolm McDonald, emeritus professor of marketing at Cranfield was appalled at the resulting lack of rigour. In his opinion, the marketing discipline had lost all respect because "lots of charlatans and halfwits had got into it without qualifications."[5]

And remember this was before the coming of the careerists who'd be pushing the purpose agenda.

In similar vein, I remember Alan Tapp, professor of marketing at Bristol Business School telling me: "If best practice has little or no value, what does? The answer is the cult of the new. In a world that lacks substance, fads and fashions take over and marketers are obsessed with the next big thing."[6]

Little did we know how damaging "the next big thing" was going to be.

Markets collapse - digital booms

Alan Tapp was giving me his gloomy prognosis back in 2008, just as adland was being plunged into further turmoil by the world financial crisis.

After the collapse of the stock market and during the recession of 2008, ad spending was cut by 10-21% across all channels.[7] Back then advertising was still largely dominated by linear communications (radio, television commercials, print, posters, etc.). Given above-the-line advertising's often cavalier approach to tracking results, little of this was measurable.

In times of economic downturn, (as we'll also see when we hit the post-Covid world later on) the C-suite suddenly takes an interest in where their chief marketing officer has been spending the money.

With little hard evidence to prove ROI on the posters, telly and print ads they'd commissioned, the CMOs became even more enamoured of digital's below-the-line claims to effectiveness.

As it looked like the lights were going out on capitalism, advertising budgets were scrutinised and reallocated. Peter Field tells us that in 2008 online advertising revenue grew by about 20%. "Overall, advertising spend held steady, but it was the start of a dramatic drift to short-term activation media, something that has cost businesses dearly over the years since then."[8]

In other words, the strategically planned, long-term brand building campaigns that are exemplified, again, by the likes of Tango, Hamlet, Lynx, Guinness and Barclaycard were abandoned. And in their place came one-off tactical executions aimed at a quick sell.

Or, as we're about to see, films that had no element of "sell" in them at all. Instead their aim was to attach the client's brand name to a trending social/political issue/problem in order to, ostensibly, boost what became known as the company's Environmental, Social and Governance credentials.

From Glasto to Croydon

All of which diminished the Creative Agencies' role as a respected business partner. Their account handlers and strategists, who'd once sat at the top table with their clients, were now kept waiting outside the boardroom while the digital shops ate their lunch.

An industry that had been part of the warp and weft of popular culture was now becoming sidelined. Indeed, with the fragmentation of available media, advertising was being literally forced to the margins of the TV schedules

Where once a TV ad might be seen by 20 million viewers on one of just three commercial channels (ITV, Channel 4 and 5) there were now dozens of commercial stations with much smaller, discrete audiences.

With clients' media budgets cut to the bone, planners were suddenly suggesting more targeted campaigns that might only be seen by a minuscule audience on Channel 42.

Which meant the rock stars of advertising had swapped Glastonbury's Pyramid Stage for Croydon's Fairfield Hall.

But just as the hits were drying up, and the crowds were drifting away, the chance of a come-back hove into view. And again the 2008/9 financial crisis was the catalyst - although this time in the most circuitous kind of way.

Remember Occupy Wall St?

It all started back in September 2011 as a small-scale demonstration in Manhattan's financial district by contributors to the Canadian political magazine, *Adbuster.* Its message: "We are the 99%" was designed to appeal to everyone who objected to the other 1% owning most of the money, property and power.

In a society still recovering from the fallout from the banking crisis, the slogan worked. And, over the coming weeks, the encampment swelled to thousands in New York and inspired similar sit-ins in over 900 cities throughout the world.

For a moment capitalism seemed to be facing an existential crisis. But then responded, as it always does, by adapting.

Momentum for the reset came from a *Harvard Business Review* article, "Creating Shared Value", which argued that businesses could still make money whilst addressing societal issues.[9] Quickly thereafter, the emphasis shifted from Milton Friedman's focus on serving the shareholder to a more progressive responsibility to the stakeholder, and what became known as the triple bottom line: "People, Planet, Profit."

This commitment became institutionalised when the Business Roundtable - the most powerful and well organised capitalist lobby in America - issued its "Statement on the Purpose of a Corporation". The defensiveness that motivated its adoption was plain to see in this introductory paragraph:

"Yet we know that many Americans are struggling. Too often hard work is not rewarded, and not enough is being done for workers to adjust to the rapid pace of change in the economy. If companies fail to recognize that the success of our system is dependent on inclusive long-term growth, many will raise legitimate questions about the role of large employers in our society."[10]

ESG to the rescue

Of course, the people with most reason to be defensive were the denizens of Wall Street who moved deftly to link investor risk and financial return to factors that are now familiar to us as Environmental, Social and Governance (ESG).

From then on ESG was promoted as the way to steer capitalism towards social impact - whilst also delivering on the bottom line. It was an alluring argument and one which became even more appealing when McKinsey published an article that apparently proved that you didn't have to rob mercantile Peter to pay altruistic Paul.[11]

As some sceptics have since pointed out, the data used to establish ESG as the driver of financial outperformance was correlational. Does a company perform better financially because it has a strong commitment to ESG? Or does the underlying infrastructure that gives companies the headroom to invest in ESG also account for the strong financial performance. In other words, is ESG a luxury that only the more successful businesses can afford?[12]

At the time, no one bothered to ask. It was, after all, McKinsey. So who would have the temerity to question them? Or suggest they might be using the research as a marketing tool for their own ESG consultancy?

With the emergence of ESG, the insurrection threatened by Occupy was scuppered. The rampant capitalism that had brought about the crash of 2008/9 was, by 2014/15, replaced by the woke variety.

And, with Tom Wolfe's "Masters of the Universe" turning into its saviours, those who wanted to operate in business had to play by their new rules.

Adland finds its purpose

Suppliers had to provide the details of their own commitment to ESG. Some found it onerous. The big players in adland, however, were only too happy with the idea that advertising had a societal role to play. The commercial purpose that had previously been the basis for strategic thinking was now coupled with a none too complementary idea: social purpose.

Indeed the two were, in many cases, incompatible. But that didn't bother a politically progressive adland. And, over the next 10 years, the industry happily shifted its attention away from selling stuff to focussing on saving the world.

Just as those on Wall Street had made the transition to woke capitalism for their own self-interest, many in the ad industry enthusiastically embraced the mantra of good = growth because it suited them.

Not only did it allow them to tell like-minded Left-leaning friends that they'd finally sloughed off the capitalist yoke. The real beauty about social purpose was it gave adland its own purpose - and a new significance at a time when it was drifting ever further to the margins of British culture.

Indeed, the great irony is that, as the ads became culturally irrelevant, we loftily ascribed to ourselves a societal role and influence far greater than any we'd previously ever dreamed of.

3
Why adland
leans Left

I ended the last chapter by referring to adland's politically progressive predilections, and noted how important they were in steering the industry towards social purpose.

But to what degree was that leaning so inclined?

Well, for example, the research done by Andrew Tenzer and Ian Murray for their white paper "The Empathy Delusion" indicated that the industry was almost twice as likely as the mainstream to align Leftwards.[1]

Many people in advertising, I'd suggest, subscribe to the social democratic ideals of the traditional centre-Left. They're temperate, politically none too dogmatic and constitute the industry's majority.

Or should I say, the industry's *silent* majority.

In today's febrile attention economy, the opinion of a minority of voluble activists, fellow travellers and careerists has predominated, and been falsely presented by our press, institutions and corporate classes as though it was the unquestionable consensus.

And what are their views?

Well, to a socialist like Ian Murray, these advertising folk simply aren't the right kind of Left-wing. As he has intimated, they are "ideologically ignorant."[2]

I suppose he means they don't adhere to Karl Marx's view that political systems are the product of economic interests. Nor are they too concerned about collective rather than private ownership of the means of production, or the root and branch redistribution of wealth from the rich to the poor. And, perhaps, most significantly, they are no longer the party of and for the working class.

For them, the enemy is still capitalism but now race/privilege and not class/economics has become the principal frame through which politics and history are understood.[3]

To reach this conclusion, they've borrowed a belief system directly from the US that has little relevance to the situation here in the UK.[4] The fight is now for the rights of our black minority plus, selectively, those of Asian and other ethnicities, women, the LGBTQ+ community and thereafter any other identity that suffers at the hands of a white, male Patriarchy.

Today's Labour Party membership is, like the ad industry, largely made up of white, middle class people. And like adland's leaders, has bought into this identitarian view of society's problems - and how they can be fixed.

We'll discuss the consequences of all this in greater detail in Part 2. Suffice to say, to socialists of the old school, this looks like the rearranging of deckchairs while the good ship Plutocracy goes sailing on.

If that's the case, then adland has more than its fair share of willing deckchair attendants.

We are the epitome of the progressive, metropolitan elite

Let's start with "elite:"

Some 70% of adlanders grew up in a household where the chief income earner was social grade AB - versus 29% of the modern mainstream.[5]

63% have parents with a professional background - versus a 37% national average.[6]

18% come from a C2DE background.[7]

91% of marketers and 72% of advertising professionals have a university degree.[8]

19% of UK advertising professionals attended fee-paying schools versus a national average of 7%.[9]

And 69% of those from a BAME background were privately educated.[10]

How about "metropolitan" and "Left-leaning?"

According to the most recent figures, nearly 32,000 people work for the big six global agency groups, and 27,000 or around 85% work in London.

That means some 90% of WPP staff, 90% of Omnicom's staff, and 95% of Publicis Groupe's staff work in the capital.[11]

That survey was taken in 2020. Since then sterling work has been done by VCCP with the Academy it opened in Stoke.[12] And other London-based networks have also bolstered their regional offerings. However, it is unlikely that the above percentage figures have been affected by any large scale relocations up north.

Of course there's been the shift toward working from home. But just because you're not based on Shoreditch every day, doesn't mean you've escaped the gravitational pull of cosmopolitan life.

As to Left-leaning, that tendency is inevitable given our industry's demographics.

Fully 73% of the agency workforce is aged 18-40, and there are no prizes for guessing that age group's political orientation.[13]

At the July, 2024 general election, voters aged 18-39 went 44% Labour, 15% Lib/Dem and 13% Green. Which means over 72% voted for Left-leaning parties.[14]

Adland actually tilted even further. *The Drum* magazine's industry exit poll showed that 79.8% voted for those Left and Left/Centre parties. And if you throw in the SNP and The Workers Party it came to 84.8%.

With just 4% voting Tory.[15]

I imagine even those findings were a conservative reflection of political life in some of London's big creative agencies.

No wonder they vote that way

You can understand why these young folk wanted to turf out the Tories. Those Millennials and Gen-Zers had seen little personal benefit from 14 years of Conservative rule or the free market economics they were nominally promoting.

Wages had stagnated since the financial crisis of 2008/9.[16] And while their Boomer parents enjoyed an unprecedented level of affluence, Millennials - aged 25-34 - had abjectly failed to make the incremental generational gains that characterised the previous 100 years of social and economic progress.

The Boomers, for example, were the beneficiaries of the property owning democracy nurtured by prime minister Margaret Thatcher in the 1980s. With continued support throughout the Blair years, home ownership peaked at just over 73% in 2007.[17]

But today, when it comes to buying a home of their own, the under 35s have more chance of handcuffing a ghost.

Whereas 50 years ago, a typical house cost just over £5,000 - the equivalent of £50,000 in today's money - the average UK house price is £270,000.[18] That's steep enough. But those who are working in a London-centric industry like advertising have to find way over twice that amount - on average £567,000 - if they want a property of their own.[19]

Home ownership offers the most fundamental stake in any society. And if you are foreclosed from that, the natural tendency is to blame the system. And, after 14 years of Tory rule, in this case, move politically Leftward.

Then there's the impact of education

As I pointed out above, 72% of advertising and 91% of marketing personnel have a university degree. Which means our industry exhibits the classic outcome of the "university divide" - i.e. distinctly different voting patterns between graduates and non-graduates.

At the July 2024 general election, a YouGov poll showed that 66% of those with a degree or higher voted Left or Centre-Left as opposed to 41% of those at a GCSE or lower level of education.[20]

Incidentally, of those attending university at the time of the election, the imbalance was even greater, with 75% leaning Leftwards.[21]

Which brings us to the contentious issue of what the youngsters who go to "uni" are being taught before they become this year's tranche of adland's graduate recruits. And if they're indoctrinated by the experience?

It seems that university faculty life is a mix of agitation and activism with a touch of deplatforming and even violence for good measure. The June 2025 YouGov report "Freedom of Speech in Higher Education" revealed that 5% of all academics surveyed are fearful of actual physical attack from people who disagree with their views.[22]

Last December a survey by *Times Higher Education* also found university staff were under pressure to keep quiet. "One British psychology academic explained that it was increasingly difficult to argue with any position deemed contentious by activists, on topics that touch upon gender, colonialism, the Israel-Palestinian conflict and neurodiversity because 'any diversion from the accepted line is seen as meaning you are a bad person rather than just someone who disagrees'".[23]

This supports the findings of Matthew Goodwin, formerly professor of politics at the University of Kent, which indicate that academics in the social sciences and humanities lean strongly Left, many are biased against Conservatives, and the latter are massively self-censoring.[24]

This impacts our industry because most of our graduates read, yes, social sciences and humanities - disciplines dominated by Critical Theory and its progressive permutations. You may think this has Foucault to do with advertising but those influenced by CT emerge - to a greater or lesser degree - with an aversion to the capitalist free enterprise system that our industry is supposed to lubricate and drive.

Many, however, avoid the day-to-day task of selling the clients' goods and services. Instead they find their natural home amongst the Diversity, Equity + Inclusion managers who now make up a sizeable faction within adland's HR departments.

DE+I 101

As students, many will have been schooled in how that role should be performed.

Here's one example of the indoctrination to which they'd have been exposed. It comes from Cardiff University which has recently made a "EDI Awareness Module" compulsory for all first-year students.

It starts with a quiz to "explore [their] experiences of privilege and marginalisation" and to impress upon them the advantages they enjoy or the discrimination they suffer in the UK's unjust, racist society.

From there they move onto a section on "microaggressions". Apparently if you believe in meritocracy and the benefits of hard work you'd better keep quiet because a comment like "Everyone can succeed if you just work hard enough" is regarded as a no-no. The same goes for voicing the opinion that "All lives matter" as, one assumes, this is regarded as a sacrilegious riposte to Black Lives Matter.

When it comes to "inclusive language", participants are taught the rules of ED+I Newspeak. It seems many English idioms are "based in ableism" such as "the blind leading the blind" and must therefore be avoided. Colloquial phrases like "kill two birds with one stone" or "piece of cake", are also out because they are "very British English" and might not be immediately understood by people from other countries.[25]

Clearly the idea that new arrivals might be encouraged to integrate with the majority culture by learning such idioms and phrases has been rejected. The pressure is upon the indigenous British to censor themselves.

It is, in short, Critical Theory 101. The aim being to encourage the freshers to read oppressive power dynamics into every aspect of student life - and to warn them that everything they say can be policed.

This is the ideology that our graduates carry over into our industry. And while most will not be fully committed, it will have shaped their attitudes and assumptions. A minority, however, will be determined to spread its reductive, discriminatory and divisive doctrine.

We'll be meeting them in Part 2.

Left-leaning cultural capitalists

There's also the argument that says our Left-leaning bias is inevitable given the fact that, as Harry Enfield's comic character had it "we're considerably richer than yow."

As we've seen, adlanders are likely to have affluent parents. According to the Institute of Practitioners in Advertising 2025 survey, we're not short of a bob or two ourselves.

An executive can expect between a minimum and maximum average annual salary of £22,000 and £45,000. For a manager it's £29,000 and £75,000, and for a head of department, £67,000 - £184,000.

And those with a seat on the board, can pull in anything from £126,000 a year and upwards.[26]

Such wealth elevates them above the concerns and goals shared by the mass of people in the UK. Those poorer folks are concerned with security and basic material comfort. To use the vernacular: "putting bread on the table"; "keeping the wolf from the door" and "making ends meet." All of which have been difficult as economic stagnation has led to non-existent growth in real wages over the past 15 years.

Aside from a wish to put sourdough bread on the table, the better off have transcended such aspirations. Establishing and maintaining status is now the priority.

In the past, possessions did the necessary signalling. But today's elites are too righteously self-aware to embrace the vulgarity of conspicuous consumption. They have instead found that a well advertised support for trending progressive causes differentiates them from the hoi polloi.

The danger of luxury beliefs

It was political commentator, Rob Henderson, who coined the term "luxury beliefs" and explained that they're dangerous because they "confer status on the upper class at very little cost, while often inflicting costs on the lower classes."[27]

To start with, ordinary people are blocked from joining the progressive elite by the intentionally exclusive terminology they use. As Henderson observed: "Your typical working class American could not tell you what 'heteronormative' or 'cisgender' means. But if you visit an elite university, you'll find plenty of affluent people who will eagerly explain them to you. When someone uses the phrase 'cultural appropriation', what they are really saying is, 'I was educated at a top college'. Only the affluent can afford to learn strange vocabulary, because ordinary people have real problems to worry about."[28]

In our industry, the damage is done when these luxury beliefs inform the advertising we create. For instance the people who worked on Always Platinum tampons thought it was a good idea to feature an obese female figure-skater in one of their TV spots. [29]

Of course this ticked the progressive boxes for body positivity, inclusivity and empowerment. However, in celebrating size XXL, the ad was also telling the world that obesity is OK - and can even itself be aspirational.

Which is fine with the middle classes and their appetite for kimchi and chia, and their patronage of the $6.3 trillion global Wellness industry.[30] But it's not a message that our poorest fellow citizens really should be ingesting. Because they are also ingesting a diet that is piling on the processed foods and bringing on the high blood pressure, type 2 diabetes and coronary heart disease that is killing them in droves.[31]

Obviously we must treat those who are deemed medically overweight with the respect they deserve. But we don't owe them a denial of reality just so we can achieve our own short-term sugar rush of moral-gratification.

Speaking of morals...

Adland's unbalanced morality

The search for status described above is a conscious choice. But there's yet another reason why adlanders push social justice. In this case it proceeds from their subconscious system of values.

In "The Empathy Delusion", their study of the values of those who work in our industry, Andrew Tenzer and Ian Murray showed that adland is overwhelmingly influenced by the "Individualising" tendency.[32]

They were basing their conclusions on Moral Foundations Theory which was co-developed by Jonathan Haidt and Jesse Graham and popularised in Haidt's book *The Righteous Mind: Why Good People are Divided by Politics and Religion*.[33]

As Haidt explained, there are five broad moral dichotomies that inform most human relationships:

1) Care or Harm
2) Fairness or Cheating
3) Loyalty or Betrayal
4) Authority or Subversion
5) Purity or Desecration.

By reconciling these dualities, mankind has created the socialising systems that enable us to survive and thrive.

Care and Fairness are regarded as "Individualising Values" and these promote kindness, gentleness, justice and respect for others' rights.

Then there are the "Binding Values" of loyalty, authority and purity which promote self-discipline, reciprocity, social solidarity, respect for authority and maintenance of community.

The point here is that while the attitudes and behaviour of those of a conservative bent are informed by all five foundations, Left-leaning progressives are not as stable. They are literally "leaning" because theirs is a morality based on an exaggerated emphasis on Care and Fairness.

Differing views on "Fairness"

Conservatives and progressives share values associated with "Fairness". But as research led by professor Mohammed Atari, director of the Culture and Morality Lab at the University of Massachusetts, Amhurst, discovered they manifest in quite different ways.

Conservatives are concerned with what professor Atari terms: "Proportionality" or "individuals getting rewarded in proportion to their merit or contribution."

Progressives, however, do not believe in this kind of meritocracy. They argue for "equality" based on "equal treatment and equal outcome for individuals."[33]

We'll see the seismic impact of "equal outcome for individuals" when, in Part 2, we discuss the meaning of equity.

But let's return our focus to an industry that is overwhelmingly concerned with Care and Fairness. And how this does much to explain the unquestioning embrace of social purpose as the go-to-market strategy for London's biggest agencies, and the abiding fixation with social justice.

Rattling the stick against the swill bucket

Both phenomena suggest a workforce at odds with the commercial reality of what had previously been the industry's *raison d'etre:* selling stuff.

For many, the free market exchange of goods and services which advertising promotes had become too red blooded in its pursuit of profit. Those on the Left struggled to find too much in the way of the "Caring" and "Fairness" we discussed above. Indeed, to many it had become synonymous with a decidedly uncaring exploitation of workers in the developing world and, worse still, despoliation of the environment.

To justify participation, activists and careerists decided advertising's role only became defensible when aligned with a trending social or environmental cause.

That certainly came across in this, at the time (2021) brave, critique by Vicki Maguire, formerly the chief creative officer at Havas London:

"Advertising's obsession with 'purpose' could tell you as much about the psyche of the people that work in advertising as it does about the marketing landscape. Have those of us embarrassed about 'rattling the stick against the swill bucket' finally found our bragging rights? If we sell conscience rather than a product or service and do it enough, will people stop thinking of us as nefarious gatekeepers of capitalism and we can go to work saving the planet one purpose at a time?"

Vicki was speaking about "the privileged public-school-educated, white executives in the industry" who made no secret of their political sympathies and, indeed, made every effort to broadcast them.[34]

In fact, as we're about to see, many of adland's most influential people were determined to use the platform that their status gave them in order to advertise their progressive views, frame the narrative and control the argument.

4
Advertising and activism

Their most prominent stage was the industry trade paper, *Campaign*.

At peak-purpose, it was delivering a daily diet of news with a hefty side order of progressive politics.

Let's take, for example, the print issue for January 2021.

We had just experienced our first nine months of Covid. And as the issue came out we were going into the second lockdown, the economy was on life support and there seemed no end to the worst global epidemic since Spanish Flu 100 years ago.

Yet in our trade paper, the deaths of over 73,000 people in England and Wales shared top billing with the murder of a man 5,000 miles away in Minneapolis.

In fact, it was apparent that many of the issue's contributors were more concerned with what senior journalist, Gemma Charles, had called "the other defining issue of 2020": the emergence of Black Lives Matter (BLM) and the galvanising effect it had had on their own activism.[1]

You got a sense of *Campaign's* editorial stance from "2020 Vision", and the six full colour spreads chosen to represent the passing year. Three related to the epidemic. The other three were of the black screen that virtually every agency ran in solidarity with BLM in the aftermath of George Floyd's murder; the toppling of the "17th century merchant and slave trader", Thomas Colston's statue in Bristol; and a triumphant Joe Biden and Kamala Harris who "made history as the first women and person of colour in the post" of vice-president.[2]

Kamala was clearly top of mind with one of the contributors to "The Year Ahead" - the special feature that asked "the industry's finest what they think is on the cards as we approach 2021."[3]

Lucy Jameson, founder of Uncommon Creative Studio reckoned "We need to think like Megan Rapinoe, Marcus Rashford and Kamala Harris. Ferocious caring needs to come to the fore. As strategists, our job is to help pave the way for a different reaction. We have the chance to influence more than the brand's voice, we can influence its actions, too."[4]

Thus we had the head of perhaps London's most admired agency saying we should bring to our jobs the progressive thinking epitomised by Kamala Harris. And yes that's the Kamala Harris whose progressive thinking put off enough US voters to guarantee the truth-bending, pussy-grabbing, quite possibly treasonous, four times convicted felon Donald Trump's resounding victory in the 2024 presidential election.

Spending the client's money to promote your own views

For Sheryl Marjoram, the then CEO of McCann, London, Kamala Harris's politics were probably way too moderate. Under her own heading: "Advertising and activism" she wrote: "There is a moral and commercial imperative here. There has been a power imbalance for centuries. Brands that recognise the platform they have to engage with consumers in a meaningful way, who have a clear and admirable purpose and do the right thing, will win".[5]

Note that this is her own "moral and commercial imperative". She wasn't speaking on behalf of her clients - and certainly for very few of the people shopping for the detergent, cereals or cosmetics that McCann was being paid to advertise. No, this was the CEO of a network agency acting like the head of a Left wing NGO, and shamefacedly advocating the use of her client's money to promote her own political views.

All this was necessary because, as Fura Johannesdottir the chief design officer at Huge told us, there was "so much at stake - from political turmoil: the need to focus on systemic racism via the Black Lives Matter movement ... to the urgent need to face the future of our planet.[6]

The need for urgency was not lost on Emma Chui, global director of intelligence at Wunderman Thompson. She was sure that, "People's increasingly ethical values are prompting brands to do better.

Brands and marketers need to step up and help build a better future for all."[7]

Yes, all the boxes were being ticked with little or no consideration of their clients' objectives. Or the clients' customers' needs.

This was their – and adland's – agenda. And one driven, I'd suggest, by another major news event that occurred several months before either the murder of George Floyd or the outbreak of Covid 19.

The progressive resistance movement

In December 2019, there was a general election in the UK, the result of which must have been anathema to the people I've quoted above. The Conservatives romped home with 365 seats to Labour's 202.

It was the latter's worst performance since 1934 and, in the aftermath, pundits were predicting that the Left would be out of power in the UK for a decade or more.

When, in 2016, the American Left suffered a similar seismic shock with the election of Donald Trump, the resistance quickly erupted.[8] Protests took place in at least 52 American cities, and business leaders, celebrities, academics and large swathes of the country's west and east coast populations promised to continue the fight until the status quo could be re-established at the next presidential election four years later.

Back in the UK in 2019, there was little mass reaction. But while no one took to the streets, the progressive elites quietly used whatever influence they had to change the culture and correct the downstream political mistakes of an electorate who'd fallen for Boris Johnson's duplicitous charms.

Making cultural transformation happen

And so, twelve months later, whilst the economic impact of Covid was biting in earnest, and clients and customers were worrying about the rising rate of inflation and a looming cost of living crisis, many of adland's C-Level remained oblivious.

They were still fighting their own private culture war.

In the 2021/22 version of *Campaign's* "The Year Ahead" we had Peter Semple, chief brand officer, Depop talking about "holding government and brands alike to account." He was also telling us "Brand purpose and values are more commercially important than ever." As were "Authentic action, integrity, foresight and progressive values."[9]

Katie Mackay-Sinclair, a partner at Mother was looking forward to "Radically changing the mindset not just of consumers we engage but across the corporate and political realm too."[10]

Then there was Lori Meakin, the founder of Joint: "We can help our clients have positive impacts on society and on their business. Whether it's social justice, wellbeing or sustainability."[11]

Natalie Graeme, a founder of Uncommon Creative Studio, wanted us to "Use our incredible creativity as an industry to engineer a different future."[12]

Ella Dolphin, chief executive of the Stylist Group was looking forward to "working differently, thinking differently and the opportunity to work with brands that really care and can make meaningful change."[13]

While joint chief executive at Adam & Eve/DDB, Tammy Einav announced "Our creative output has a huge role to play in influencing behavioural, attitudinal and societal shifts in terms of diversity, sustainability and equality. We will do more to capitalise on our ability - and responsibility - to not just be part of a cultural transformation, but also to make it happen".[14]

And, from the client side we had Unilever's Aline Santos chipping in with "Brands must have a point of view, but more importantly must take action to drive real change."[15]

Social engineering to the progressive blueprint

I'm sorry if I've laboured the point here, but it is a crucial one. Not only were the individuals quoted above allowed to use the industry's foremost trade publication to advertise their political views. They were also describing the mindset they'll have encouraged and, through force of personality and policy, probably promoted to those who worked under them.

All this talk of "meaningful change" ... "influencing behavioural, attitudinal and societal shifts" ... "cultural transformation" ... "driving real, lasting change" ... "engineering a different future" ... "radically changing the mindset" had nothing to do with the agency's day job i.e. radically changing a shopper's brand preference and the things they throw in their trolley.

The change described here was social and cultural engineering to the progressive blueprint. And the aim was to educate the public about race, multiculturalism, gender, sexual orientation and the climate crisis.

This was our industry leaders' agenda. The fact that they were the self-appointed arbiters of what needed to change and no one had asked them to engineer that "different future" never seemed to occur to them. Nor was their astounding arrogance commented upon by the industry magazine's editorial staff.

All concerned were demonstrating the progressive gaze at its most intense. And what an exhilarating almost transcendent feeling it must have been.

The African-American social theorist, Thomas Sowell refers to this way of interpreting the world as, not the gaze but "The Vision." And says it offers "a special state of grace for those who believe in it. Those who accept the vision are deemed to be not merely factually correct but morally on a higher plane. Put differently, those who disagree with the prevailing vision are seen as being not merely in error, but in sin."[16]

Advertising's progressive elite were "The Vision's" unimpeachable champions. They were absolutely convinced they were doing the "right thing". And why not?

As an article alongside 2020's "The Year Ahead" pointed out: "Progress is not just profit. Doing the right thing is now a key measure of progress."[17]

Beamed direct from the right side of history

"Doing the right thing" was something of a fixation with Tim Lindsay, the long-time leader of one of adland's most influential institutions, D&AD.

In a revealing podcast with the freelance writer, Ben Kay, Tim positioned himself in the vanguard of a crusade formed of "all the good people", "the coalition of the willing" and "people like us".[18]

Indeed, if you listen to this *folie à deux,* just count the number of times Tim describes his choice of action as "the right thing to do".

Like many progressive leaders, he was swift to reassure us that his message was being beamed direct from "the right side of history". And, clearly, from this vantage point, alternate opinion (if there was any) could be met with a dismissive shrug.

Indeed, there's one moment when Ben has the good grace to say: "There's a lot of Steve Harrison's perspective out there. There are a lot of people who say we should be selling. Not only is this purpose thing a distraction but it is damaging to advertising at a time when it's, if not on its knees then, in a somewhat more submissive position than it has ever been."

Tim eventually offered this riposte: "I am very keen to keep pushing this agenda forward, despite what people like Steve may feel and think. There are people like him in the business who think this is just Lefty nonsense. But I don't really care about that anymore."

As he concluded, "the aim is to normalise the right kind of behaviour".[19]

And who would be defining "the right kind of behaviour"?

Well, Tim of course.

"Our main responsibility is to inspire bravery"

The belief that advertising's Left-leaning luminaries should be defining "the right kind of behaviour" wasn't limited to the UK industry. It was a global phenomenon.

The above quotes came, as I said, when belief in purpose was at its height. But even in 2023, when questions were being asked, there was still an evangelical zeal amongst its advocates. In March of that year *Little Black Book* asked "How Should Brands Navigate the Culture War" and got these kind of responses:

Doctor Rodney Collins, the director of McCann Worldgroup's global intelligence unit Truth Central was still convinced that "People around the world have increased expectations that brands and businesses will not only fulfil their functional offering but also play a social, even a political, role ... Taking seriously that to be part of culture means taking a stand in culture."[20]

"There's no avoiding any of these 'kitchen table' issues," said Megha Parikh, head of strategy at Wunderman Thompson, Atlanta, "Ultimately, I remind myself that the core of our job, our main responsibility is to inspire bravery."[21]

Siona Singletary, associate strategy director at R/GA Australia was also of the opinion that: "Brands are expected to take sides on contentious issues. Ignoring the 'culture war' can be a missed opportunity to connect with consumers and more importantly to drive change, because brands hold power."[22]

Amy Travis, creative director at BBH USA spoke of giving brands "the opportunity to start a new conversation, shape behaviours, drive action, and change culture for the better."[23]

As with Tim Lindsay's "right kind of behaviour" you were left in no doubt that changing culture "for the better" would be done to Amy's progressive specification.

"Alienated from the lived experience"

You'll note, from the above comments, how often it was the strategists who were setting the agenda. Which was unfortunate because it seems that the self-proclaimed "smartest people in the room" might not have been best qualified to do so.

This was pointed out by one of their number, Martin Weigel (who, in fact, is one of the smartest people working in the industry).

Two months after the appearance of the first *Campaign* "Year Ahead" cited above, Martin had this to say about his fellow planners: "We are disconnected from the mainstream, alienated from the lived experience of other people's realities, and vastly overestimate our ability to transcend our own experience and worldview and understand mainstream aspirations. Simply resorting to our 'intuition' and extrapolating from our own personal experiences cannot bridge that gap."[24]

Unfortunately, it wasn't just the planners who turned their backs on their audience in order to talk amongst themselves. At the time Martin's blog post appeared, the entire industry was displaying a lack of empathy for or interest in mainstream public opinion that verged on the pathological.

And why?

Because there were so few opposing voices. Only a handful of people were questioning these progressive pundits' right to speak for the industry. And even fewer were making the argument for capitalism, advertising's commercial purpose and the value that demand generation brought to a client's business.

The activists and careerists had seized the microphone. Those with an alternate point of view weren't even on the stage. In fact, forget the stage, they weren't allowed in the auditorium and were lucky if they made it into the car park.

Controlling the means of communication

What had happened here was a reflection of what was happening across the UK's media, arts and our major educational, business, political and law enforcement institutions. Where Karl Marx had emphasised the importance of seizing ownership of the means of production, his progressive heirs had taken control of the means of communication.

In advertising's case, the shift was from the factory floor to the creative department. That's where the process of normalising the right kind of behaviour would begin.

In London especially, the activists and careerists were largely unopposed by adland's rank and file. These people went with the flow knowing it would be dangerous for them to beat against the current. The same could be said for the people who ran our agencies and institutions.

But actually, in the face of dwindling commercial and cultural significance, many of them rather liked being told that the articles and speeches they were writing, the awards shows and conferences they were organising and the ads they were making were saving the planet and putting an end to racism, sexism and homophobia.

Meanwhile, their older peers announced their staunch commitment to such causes as a way of holding onto their jobs.

As we'll see, it was becoming increasingly dangerous to be "male, pale and stale". And many who answered that description made a point of loudly supporting the progressive arguments that would otherwise hasten their departure from the scene. It didn't make them entirely fireproof but it gave them a stay of execution while others were being led to the wall.

Bread and circuses

For the people at the very top, the ones who could affect real change in the industry, there was another self-interested reason for supporting progressive causes. As we'll see in greater detail in our final chapter, backing those initiatives deflected attention away from an industry in crisis.

In this case, it served *their* purpose to push purpose.

In an increasingly cash strapped industry, it was hard to placate a disgruntled crowd with bread. But the promotion of purpose - and the attention, awards and the self-congratulatory esteem it generated - provided the circus entertainment needed to distract the discontented.

For a while at least.

Which is why you had people like Mark Read, the boss of WPP, channeling his inner Tim Lindsay and telling Campaign: "Purpose starts with doing the right thing and that's what's most important."[25]

You'd have thought his clients might have suggested that building their brands and selling their products was actually of greater importance.

But you'd have been wrong.

Clients had lost their marbles, too

No one more so than Aline Santos, global marketing and chief diversity & inclusion officer at Unilever.

Here she is in her article: "Purpose is the Future of Business" in April 2021: "It is now undeniably clear that business must step up to be a force for positive change and deliver more than great products or services. Purpose is no longer an option, it's a core requirement to the future of business ... People expect brands to take active roles in social, environmental and political discussions, instigating and effecting positive social change."[26]

Aline was the purpose proponent *par excellence.* And took full advantage of the freedom and backing given by her boss, the CEO of Unilever, Alan Jope. A couple of years earlier he'd announced: "We will dispose of brands that we feel are not able to stand for something more important than making your hair shiny, your skin soft, your clothes whiter or your food tastier."[27]

The fact that consumers bought Unilever's products precisely because they made their hair shiny and their skin soft, seemed to escape Jope and Co.

And it wasn't just Unilever. The activists had also taken over at Danone and Procter & Gamble.

It's not surprising really. The marketing people on the client side had been to the same universities, inhabited the same metropolitan bubbles and shared the same progressive values and luxury beliefs as their agency counterparts.

They were also all reading the same research.

Truth is being devalued

The most influential came from Edelman, one of the world's biggest PR and marketing companies.

By asking the right questions, they got the results the proponents of purpose wanted to see. Namely, lots of Gen-Zers saying how committed they were to businesses run on ethical rather than economic lines. It wasn't just the clients and agencies who delighted in such revelations. The trade press and even the nationals duly reproduced Edelman's press releases in lieu of actually doing some real journalism.

It should be added that Edelman had its own new business targets. And the regular publication of its surveys might be seen as a tactic for achieving that growth. Those surveys being not news, but marketing ploys.

The PR expert and media commentator Mark Borkowski discussed in general terms the dangers of ignoring that distinction when he warned how "narratives are controlled, how attention is manipulated, and how truth itself is being devalued … in today's media ecosystem, who asks the question, and how they ask it, is just as important as the answer."[28]

For several years, Edelman provided the answers the CMOs wanted to hear. Which meant that, as *Marketing Week's* resident realist professor Mark Ritson observed: "our marketing knowledge base is increasingly constructed from undercooked, overstated research that is all about the headline and not about the rigour."[29]

"We have failed to prove our worth"

Those surveys and headlines "proving" widespread support for the CMO's social purpose strategies came in very handy whenever fellow C-suite colleagues got round to asking them where the marketing budget had gone.

Thankfully, there were one or two sceptics on the client side who saw the damage this was doing to both their discipline and to broader business interests. Here's Benjamin Braun, CMO, Samsung Europe:

"We have failed to prove our worth. If you ask a marketing team how many products they sold after spending X amount on a campaign, the chances are they won't be able to tell you. The majority of marketing teams at the moment would not be able to articulate their results in a way that would impress the chairman, CEO or CFO."[30]

There was a similar assessment from Raja Rajamannar, chief marketing and communications officer, Mastercard:

"When chief execs of major companies were interviewed, 70% of them said that they have zero to low confidence in their chief marketers and in their marketing teams to be able to drive business growth. Why? The fundamental reason is because when marketers are asked questions like, 'We have spent so many million dollars on these campaigns – what exactly did the company get by way of return on its investment in marketing?' Most of the time, the answers are fluffy or these folks look like deer caught in headlights."[31]

Again, we must remember that Braun and Rajamannar were lone voices. And that, aside from these Jeremiahs, most marketing people were happy to go along with the pious wishful thinking that passed for thought leadership.

And why not? Everyone was hitting their numbers. And when they weren't, the banks were making up the shortfall.

Few asked what might happen when that free credit bubble burst?

5
Post-purpose

With interest rates at zero, we'd had a decade of free money. Which meant big corporations could support a sustainable cost structure and even invest in research and development via interest-free credit.

So, at the time of peak purpose, both government and business had convinced themselves that inflation would never return and borrowing costs would be low forever.

As such, clients were under no real pressure to be self-funding via sales and organic growth, and could complacently kick any long-term policy choices into the long grass.

But then suddenly, from 0.1% in December 2021, the Bank of England's interest rate shot up to 5.25% in little more than 18 months.[1]

The reason? Soaring inflation which climbed from virtually zero in summer 2020 to hit 11.1% in October 2022 - the highest rate for 40 years.[2]

Like the interest rates which were increased to combat inflation, rising prices charged by suppliers also ate away at business profits.

When these price rises were passed onto the consumer, the rich swapped Waitrose for Lidl and Aldi while the poor swapped Poundland for shoplifting and food banks.

The resulting cost of living crisis rapidly refocussed everyone's mind. With businesses suffering soaring supplier prices, energy bills and borrowing costs, the C-suite suddenly shifted attention to the old sales curve.

Which meant taking a long overdue interest in what was going on in what had previously been referred to as "the colouring in department."

Unilever's *volte-face*

Over at Unilever, the result was organisational change that put the emphasis back on growth.

In May 2022 Unilever set up a separate Ice Cream Unit (which, incidentally, included that famously progressive brand, Ben & Jerry's).

The new unit's president, Matt Close, said the move was "exciting because it really puts accountability in the hands of the people who have a deep understanding of the business."[3]

And what those people deeply understood was that buying ice cream is an indulgent act which customers do on impulse to make themselves feel better ... happier ... comforted ... rewarded.

They tend not to do it because, in Ben & Jerry's case, the people who make the ice cream support an independent Palestinian homeland.

Julian Barraux, the CMO of the Ice Cream Unit explained: "What we say internally is we need indulgence first and foremost, and then purpose".[4]

But he then added that this won't be a political purpose, "the idea of [bringing] happiness and pleasure through its products is something the business has at its heart, and can be another way to realise purpose."[5]

From Barraux and his boss, Matt Close's comments, you sensed a collective sigh of relief reverberating through the Unilever organisation.

Throughout Alan Jope's time as CEO, they'd had to work with those who thought that moral superiority was more appealing to consumers than product superiority.

That, however, was not how the consumer saw things. Not when they could get four Magnum-like ice creams from Aldi for little more than the price of a real one.

As Jope's reign drew to a close, he too saw the need to switch priorities. In an urgent call to increasingly unimpressed investors he said "Our business groups are taking decisions more quickly and driving sharper strategic action ... We're investing more in product quality and brand support to ensure that they offer superior performance and value."[6]

"Product quality ... superior performance ... value." Within months, that message had been translated into a Magnum commercial all about the negative things buying a "fake Magnum" say about you - and why you should always "Stick to the Original."[7]

Growth comes before good

Over at P&G, Marc Pritchard was experiencing the same kind of Damascene conversion.

In June 2022 he attended the Viva Tech conference in Paris and told the delegates: "The industry in general has just gone too far into the good and potentially not paying enough attention to growth," Apparently growth now came before good. As he said, "The order matters, because first and foremost we're in business. Our job is to innovate on our products. Our growth drives economic good. Growth drives jobs. And it decides the partners you work with, the retailers you work with. And then it enables you to do more good for society and planet. Force for growth leads to being a force for good".

"Now, more than ever, double down on making sure you have superiority from a product standpoint."[8]

That about-turn was, as I said, executed in June 2022 - in the very month that Cannes hit peak purpose. Of all the Grands Prix that were awarded, some 85% went to purpose or cause-related ideas.[9]

Game changer

Sure enough, down there on the Cotes d'Azur, adland's leading players were celebrating the goals they'd scored with their political footballs. Meanwhile, the big game had moved to another pitch and was now being played by a very different set of rules.

These were explained several months later by P&G's CFO, Andre Schulten. As he told Morgan Stanley's gathering of analysts, superior products had enabled the FMCG giant to withstand competition from private label alternatives and achieve healthy growth.

He went on to explain that P&G's products had to be so noticeably better that "when you use them for the first time, you are clear that it's the best possible solution you could purchase." As Schulten continued, it was this superiority that not only drove repeat purchase, but also triggered social media "buzz" which encouraged others to buy.

In a big nudge to his agencies' strategists he concluded "with the right proposition" the consumer is willing to choose and pay for a premium product if they are "reassured it is delivering value".[10]

Clearly, we'd come a long way from the days when P&G's Marc Pritchard would give all the agencies on his roster the "Cannes Brief". The subject of which was always purpose-related and the objective always a gold Lion.[11]

But purpose still ruled at Cannes

Such self-indulgence was on the wane. And at Cannes the following year the tone was more, let's say, realistic.

Indeed the sea of sanctimony that had swamped the industry had reached its high water mark at Cannes '22. Twelve months on and the gravitational pull of economic necessity had started to turn the tide.

In the run up to Cannes, *Adweek* sensed change was in the air and reported: "Creatives are eying a shift toward business results and humor".

They were "hoping juries will enter deliberations with more scrutiny toward whether purpose-based work actually drove real results for brands" and were "looking for humor and advertising that actually sells stuff will win more of the spotlight in 2023."[12]

This hope was largely unrealised, and again social purpose held firm against its commercial counterpart.

That wasn't too surprising. Delivering a judgement in an awards jury that runs counter to the consensus is always a test of one's mettle. And in this case, it would have been especially so, given how deeply entrenched purpose had become in the industry psyche.

Moreover, creatives have never been great at explaining business metrics. And, when faced with purpose advocates and their playbook of guilt trips, moral scolding and pious platitudes, someone arguing for work that simply sold a product wouldn't have the political vocabulary, rehearsed rhetoric or nerve to try and win the room over.

"Your job is to sell shit"

There was, however, one highly persuasive dissident at the festival. And he certainly had enough chutzpah to speak out.

It's worth noting that the uber famous guest speakers often set the tone for that year's festival. For example, the whole purpose circus had kicked off back in 2012 when the ringmaster was former President Bill Clinton.

He'd urged the ad industry to use its formidable powers of communication and persuasion to solve the world's most pressing problems which he identified as "climate change, gender equality and personal empowerment."[13]

Fast forward to 2023 and it was left to film director Spike Lee to tell his audience the buttock-clenchingly inconvenient truth that: "The priority is to make as much money [for brands] as [you] can. If you're in a position where you don't do that, then you'll get fired."

He added: "This is the trick – how can you be creative [and] at the same time make work that drives product and sales?

"I think we all have to be honest, your job is to sell soap, soup, fast food, electronics. Your job is to sell shit, by hook or [by] crook."

In case that message hadn't got through, he closed with "the number-one aim is you've got to sell shit."[14]

At which I imagine most of the audience took a sudden and intense interest in the top of their shoes.

The intellectual challenge to purpose

The thing to note here is that once it had been questioned, purpose had few real champions. By that I mean individuals who were willing or able to make the intellectual or business argument on its behalf.

This was possibly because their claims had gone unchallenged for years. So they'd never had to develop a response much beyond a 280 character tweet or a cut 'n' stick chart from the latest Edelman survey.

With typical acuity, Bob Hoffman had described the arguments made by advocates of social purpose as "comfortable banalities that evolve into unquestionable truths."[15]

For ten years we heard them from our biggest brands and agencies, and our most influential trade papers and industry institutions.

What they said was "true" because they wanted it to be "true". Little empirical evidence was given. The mere assertion that they were doing "the right thing" was usually sufficient.

So, to bring its flimsy arguments down, all it took was a bit of intellectual rigour and some illuminating stats.

The first was offered by the doyen of planners, Paul Feldwick. It's Feldwick's contention that advertising's roots lie with the hucksters, hawkers and barkers who pulled the punters and pushed their wares by being entertaining.

It was their schtick that made them stand out from the crowd and their message memorable. As Paul explained, we are heirs to these showmen. And if we want to grab attention and get our audience to engage, we must realise that advertising works best when it is upbeat and fun.

All this was explained and expanded upon in his brilliant book *Why Does the Pedlar Sing?* The overall message to the industry being: after 12 years of hyper-seriousness, we'd better lighten up.[16]

We're in showbusiness

This chimed well with the work being done by System 1, the testing/research group whose own schtick is "predicting the short and the long term commercial potential of ads and ideas."[17]

Two of its major players, Jon Evans and Orlando Wood had always been purpose sceptics. Indeed, when the purpose bubble showed the first sign of deflating back in Sept 2022 Jon told *Campaign* "The centre of gravity has moved away from 'is this creative going to work and deliver results?', to 'is this creative going to change society?' We need to rebalance the conversation ... we need to elevate the contribution that marketing has on business, on the economy and on jobs."[18]

Meanwhile, Orlando was writing a couple of books which, in a round and about way, blamed much of advertising's creative recent failings on left-brained, Left-leaning didactic puritanism.[19]

Through System1's Funometer, they were able to "prove" time and again that tickling people's ribs was more commercially effective than jabbing your finger in their chest. Po-faced purpose was a big turn-off. People wanted a laugh, not a lecture.

With clients ever more cautious and agencies just as unsure about their true role and abilities, System 1's conjectures took on the authority of holy writ. And suddenly there were few people willing to challenge this new orthodoxy.

Relentless

Likewise there weren't many people willing to naysay Nick Asbury when he brought out his forensic dismantling of the argument for purpose.

His book, *The Road to Hell,* launched in May 2024 and thereafter he ran a relentless campaign of LinkedIn posts, articles, podcasts and speeches to challenge the purpose belief system.[20]

Nick's persuisive power lies not merely in his thoroughness, but also his ability to sound reasonable whilst exposing the fatuousness of his opponents' argument. His own Left-leaning sensibility also deflects criticism from those who'd otherwise damn his critique as Right wing polemic.

Or at least most of them. But he has also suffered the vitriol of the progressive hardliners.

As he told me "most of the response was lovely – it was either highly positive or thoughtfully critical." However, there were those who, unwilling to tolerate an alternative point of view, attempted to silence him.

"There was just a small group on LinkedIn who admitted to not having read the book, but went straight to words like 'dangerous', 'misinformation' and 'Trumpian' to describe it.

"In the wake of one WARC podcast, the organiser was questioned on why I'd been 'platformed' and asked to 'more effectively screen for' people like me in future. Wherever you are in the debate, it should be obvious that this is crossing a line – it's one thing to disagree, and another to get the person deplatformed. While the attempt wasn't successful (WARC eventually clarified they welcomed my views) the intention isn't just to target that person, but to create an air of 'stay away' for anyone else. Hopefully the power of those tactics is waning."[21]

An ideology not a fad

The arguments presented by Nick, Paul Feldwick and System1 dismantled the ring fence that had protected purpose from scrutiny and criticism. As we have seen, that culminated in the obloquy and derision heaped on the progressive pretensions of the Jag film; and in one of the industry's most respected planners calling for an inquiry into how "we lost our collective marbles" over social purpose.

I'd suggest, however, that despite the precipitous collapse of the purpose argument, the progressive activists and careerists have not gone away.

Purpose is not one of advertising's fads. It is not like native or influencer advertising nor is it akin to customer relationship marketing or search engine optimisation. It is rooted in an ideology, and those who've bought into that ideology have spent over ten years embedding themselves in our institutions and hiring in their own likeness.

Those activists are there because it gives them the means of imposing the change they feel our society, economy and culture needs. Alongside them are careerists who see performative commitment to that change as a path to promotion, awards and - particularly in our institutions - a career in itself.

Are they going to give this up because their clients need to sell stuff?

'Course not.

From such vantage points they've used their influence to, as I said earlier, frame the arguments and set the agenda for the industry. They've highlighted issues that are important to them, and ignored those that aren't. They've praised actions and outcomes that further their cause, given platforms to those with whom they agree and denied them to their opponents.

The result, a systemic bias that's impacted the trade press's headlines; who's received the industry's awards and accolades; who's been hired and who hasn't; what the ads are about and even which accounts the industry is allowed to work on.

But let's begin with something so crucial it goes to the very heart of why we turn up for work every day - and why clients pay us to do so.

Let's look at D&AD, and how its leaders set about imposing a redefinition of creative excellence that served their ideological ends.

6
The long march through adland's institutions

We have already seen how D&AD's, Tim Lindsay dismissed criticism of his purpose-driven campaigning with a blithe "I am very keen to keep pushing this agenda forward, despite what people like Steve may feel and think. There are people like him in the business who think this is just Lefty nonsense. But I don't really care about that anymore."[1]

As we're about to find, the core of that agenda involved changing our very understanding of what successful advertising looks like.

Historically there were no hard and fast rules for what constituted award-winning work at D&AD, or any of the other leading gong fests.

But there was always an acceptance that the entry had shifted some product. And that it had actually run - and those that hadn't were called out as "scam".

After that, the work was judged on the quality of the idea and the skill with which it was executed. This usually meant provoking these comments: "I've never seen that done before" and "Bastards! I wish I'd done it".

But for over 10 years, D&AD - and other of adland's institutions - adjusted those criteria.

Noble cause corruption

The emphasis was shifted from brilliance in creativity and craft to work that reflected and reinforced the progressive values of those who ran the organisation.

During his tenure as CEO, Tim Lindsay made few attempts to disguise his political leanings. As noted above, buoyed by the seemingly inexorable rise of purposeful work, he went on Ben Kay's podcast in November 2020 to discuss the way forward.

They riffed on the possibility of giving awards based on a prescribed diversity quota for cast and crew. They also discussed withholding awards from automotive ads because they encouraged the burning of fossil fuels. It was a ban which, if applied retrospectively, would have ruled out the brilliant work done for the likes of VW, Honda and Volvo Trucks.

Tim also seemed to suggest that the Awards could be used to push the agenda forward - even if it involved compromising the very integrity of the competition. He accepted that they were being given to purpose driven work that "undoubtedly is a scam" and that "tick all the right boxes to win an award". And he went on to say "green washing and woke washing is actually a step in the right direction ... because it's a step on a journey that ends with people doing the right thing".[2]

To get people "doing the right thing" Tim was quick to surround himself with like-minded Lefties.

Jobs for the progressive boys

When, in 2019, he stepped sideways from CEO to chairman, he was replaced by Patrick Burgoyne who, in Tim's words, was going to "lead the charity into the next crucial phase of its journey."[3]

It was fairly obvious where that trip was heading.

Writing in *Creative Review* a month earlier, Patrick had urged agencies to embrace purpose. As he said, they needed to "be clear on their ethical stance". Which, as we'll see, was an item high on Tim's agenda.[4]

Burgoyne's journey was derailed by Covid -19 and its effect on D&AD's finances. He voluntarily stepped down in summer and immediately set up URGE which described itself as "a creative industries collective dedicated to system change."[5]

Having been a trustee of the D&AD for less than a year, Burgoyne had been fast-tracked into the role. The following year, similar corners were cut for another of D&AD's big appointments.

In an unprecedented move, D&AD president-elect Ben Terrett, suddenly stood down so the activist, Naresh Ramchandani, could take over.[6]

Naresh set the tone for his year ahead by telling *Campaign*: "Brands do have to be politically minded or at least aware."[7] And followed that with his first president's dinner: "Protest, Typography, and the Fight for Justice – Tré Seals on a Practice Rooted in Purpose".[8]

Thereafter, Naresh's activism seemed to inform all his responses to the opportunities and problems facing our industry.

The solution's purpose, now what's the problem?

For example, when *The Drum* magazine asked: "How do we solve a problem like ... attracting bright young talent". Naresh replied: "I would ask that we keep the climate crisis top of mind, always." And continued: "If we keep the climate top of mind, we'll attract young creatives who want to apply their idealism not just to this month's job or next year's award circuit, but to a world that needs imagination of the freshest and most radical kind."[9]

Which is fine if you're recruiting people to work for an NGO, Greenpeace, or a climate crisis action group.

But the article was about attracting talent to the advertising industry where the main job is selling clients' products and services to their mainstream audiences. This requires people who understand the preoccupations and priorities of those who live beyond adland's progressive, metropolitan bubble. However, like many inhabitants of that ecosystem, Naresh seemed to have convinced himself that most people shared *his* preoccupations and priorities.

Redefining creative excellence

When Tim Lindsay explained the appointment, it was as much Naresh's activism as his creative skills that seemed to have impressed. He was, as Tim said, "a strong believer in making the right ethical choices for our industry."[10]

But maybe that was because creativity had become just a function of "the right ethical behaviour". Naresh certainly seemed to think so. As he said, "the best commercial work needs to be effortlessly ethical".

That observation was made in his introduction to the 2021 D&AD Awards Annual which, to his obvious satisfaction, was dominated by purpose-driven work.

He noted that there was still some "work that simply 'sells stuff'". And explained: "It's not that I don't value this work. I do. The best of it is excellent, and excellence is always hard and should always be valued. But in my view, turning social purpose into creative excellence is harder, and should be valued more highly".[11]

And there you had it, the new, updated definition of excellence writ large in the covering essay to what most creatives view as the handbook on how to achieve creative fame and fortune.

Now you could say that was just one man's opinion. But this wasn't just any old pundit sounding off. This was the president of D&AD whose judgement was freighted with the significance and influence that came with that role.

In case anyone hadn't got the message about what they should be aiming for, it was reiterated in his valedictory essay when he explained that "Work that advances the greater good is what creative excellence is right now ... when it's done well, good intentions plus excellent execution equals brilliance and makes work that simply sells stuff pale by comparison."[12]

Little wonder then that in the year after Naresh's presidency, 2022, his favourite kind of work swept the board at D&AD. This really was the summer of peak purpose with, as we saw on page 66, 85% of Cannes Grands Prix going that way, too.

MAKE. CHANGE

By then, however, a degree of purpose fatigue was setting in, with some observers saying its dominance was damaging creative standards.

Even a purposeful soul like Tim Lindsay's old interlocutor, Ben Kay wrote: "If you want to win the highest advertising prizes you must, must, must create a piece of work that either contains, or simply is, a purpose-based initiative."[13]

He then went on Linkedin to ask if it was time to rebalance towards work with a commercial purpose. Tim's response: "We do need to have a bit of a rethink."[14]

But, with apparently not much of one. Because the galvanising headline - or, more like, the diktat - for 2023's D&AD Awards was: MAKE. CHANGE.[15]

It was a clumsy iteration of what many of adland's leaders saw as their *raison d'etre*: to change culture in line with their progressive politics.

D&AD's then CEO, Jo Jackson, indicated there'd be no change at the organisation when, in September 2023, she explained "We believe that great creative work creates better outcomes for all".[16]

Here she was simply reiterating chairman Tim's definition of the best work as that which produces "better outcomes" not just "commercially" but also "culturally, socially, politically, environmentally".[17]

To which the objective response might have been: Really? Does every winner deemed "great" have to meet the "better outcomes" criteria as defined by those who control our industry's most important award show?

What of those entries whose "better outcome" lay simply in persuading people to buy the product? And that achieved this by exemplifying the best in insight, craft skills and big ideas?

Isn't that what the awards should have been about?

No change at D&AD

It was doubtful that would ever happen while the progressive groupthink dominated the organisation.

And sure enough in 2024 *Creative Review* duly announced the awarding of four Black Pencils to work that aimed at having "a positive impact on society".[18]

D&AD trustee Kwame Taylor-Hayford told the magazine he felt that the awarded work "reflects the industry's resilience and bravery". And went on to say "In the face of so much change, the creativity awarded at the show demonstrates beautifully how we are expanding our remit far beyond communication, creating products, services, initiatives that drive brand growth, societal change and human connection."[19]

As Nick Asbury, the industry's most astute critic of social purpose observed:

"Once again, the mood music is about the resilience and bravery of an industry that is 'expanding its remit' to drive societal change. Once again, there's no sense of D&AD 'serving' the creative industry, rather than continually trying to 'shape' it from on high.

"An attitude of 'serving' would see the judges, including the Black Pencil judges, faithfully sticking to the entry criteria of excellence in craft and creativity, instead of 'this just feels important to me' chest-puffing.

"It will only ever happen if D&AD itself starts 'driving change' within its own judging panels: you're not here to be world leaders or the Vatican sending out smoke signals. You're here to judge the best creativity, whether it's for an airline, a burger or a charity. That's what our entrants paid for. We've picked you because you're experts in creativity and craft, not politics or social change." [20]

A nice thought. But would that ever happen while the people who ran D&AD were wedded to the idea that the best advertising functioned to reflect their progressive values?

Compare and contrast

When Dara Lynch took over as CEO in June 2024 it seemed unlikely. She'd been D&AD's COO for five years. So, one imagines, had been very much aware of its ideological capture.

Such doubts were born out when she announced the identity of the first president on her watch.

It was, yes, that driver of "societal change", Kwame Taylor-Hayford. As *Campaign* reported: "As president, Taylor-Hayford will focus on mentoring and advancing future creative leaders, as well as highlight the value of purpose-driven work for brands."[21]

Dara chipped in with the view that her new president: "champions diverse talent and ignites social change through creativity, reflecting D&AD's core values at their heart."[22]

It might have been a good idea had she compared the core values she mentioned with the mission statement that got the organisation its charitable status: "Education of the community by encouraging the understanding, appreciation and commission of good design and advertising in communications media of all kinds by providing, presenting, organising and managing exhibitions, publications, tours of various British and foreign cities, classes, lecturers, seminars, tutorials and other educational activities".[23]

She'd have noticed there's nothing in there about igniting social change. Yet, year after year, D&AD had acted more like an advocacy group pursuing this politicised agenda. And one that had used the awards as a means of steering the industry towards "the right kind of behaviour".

D&AD goes commercial

Changing the definition of creative excellence had been the aim. And during the years of peak purpose that seemed highly possible.

But, as we've seen, by 2025 the pendulum had swung back in favour of "work that simply sells stuff".

Across the industry, social purpose had surrendered the stage to commercial purpose. Which even those with the progressive gaze couldn't help noticing. And so, as the D&AD's website explained when it came to announce this year's winners:

"This year's judging process has marked a major evolution in D&AD's approach. Jurors emphasised the critical importance of commercial viability, seeking work that demonstrates tangible business impact and drives meaningful behavioural change rather than celebrating creativity for its own sake."[24]

The fact that rewarding work that had a commercial impact was a "major evolution" tells you just how far out on the purpose limb the people at D&AD had climbed.

In order to clarify things further, its announcement continued:

"In other words, if there was ever a danger that agencies would make work primarily to win awards rather than serve the client, that's now history."[25]

I suppose they were too shame-faced to say:

"In other words, if there was ever a danger that agencies would make scam work that won awards through some spurious association with that year's trending progressive cause, that's now history."

Or should that be, "that's now the wrong side of history?"

The IPA abandons its original purpose

D&AD turned a blind eye to the purpose entries that broke its rules.

Another of the industry's most important awards shows simply changed theirs so more of that kind of work could win.

This time it was the Institute of Practitioners in Advertising (IPA). For 40 years they had been the champion of work that worked, and every 12 months celebrated it with their prestigious Effectiveness Awards.

When the IPA launched those Awards in 1980, it was ridiculed by many who thought it impossible to measure the impact of the creative element in the whole marketing mix.

But the IPA went ahead with this as their "purpose". Yes, it used that term, but in this case it was very much a commercial purpose: Namely, "to demonstrate that advertising can be proven to work against measurable criteria, for example, sales measures and show that it is both a serious commercial investment and a contribution to profit, not just a cost."

It then set itself two challenges: "First, to prove that advertising could add value and demonstrably contribute to profit and, second, in doing so to develop and spread best practice."[27]

Fast forward 40 years and when all other award shows were showering social purpose entries with gongs, the IPA's was a beacon of sound business sense.

And, amidst the bias and scamming, it was keeping the industry honest.

Creating your own definition of success

But then, in 2022, the people who were running the industry's most respected show suddenly changed tack. To attract more social purpose entries to its Effectiveness Awards and increase their chances of winning, the IPA amended the entry criteria.

As "Effective on Purpose", its report into why the change was happening, explained: "The criteria have evolved from calculating the financial return of brand activity to the broader one of demonstrating 'value creation'. This term frees entrants to qualify this value in the most appropriate terms."[28]

The nebulous term "value creation" meant they no longer had, to quote the award show's founding aim, "to show that it is both a serious commercial investment and a contribution to profit, not just a cost."

In effect, entrants would be allowed to make up their own definition of success.

In defending this decision, Harjot Singh, the IPA's convenor of judges at that year's awards reiterated: "The advantage of the term 'value creation' is that it is broad enough to enable entrants to make the case for the kind of value they created".

He went on to say it was now necessary, "If the brand and activity in question were not driven by a financial return or worse, where financial calculations were likely to be highly approximate or even insensitive."[29]

Note that last bit. Then ask yourself when did we become so far removed from the commercial imperative that discussing the "financial calculations" might be deemed "insensitive"?

Either way he was, I assume, saying that campaigns with non-commercial objectives would now be able to compete on level terms.

Which was an argument he then proceeded to destroy a few paragraphs later when he said "For decades they [the Awards] have also rewarded work that shifted the behaviour of smokers, motorists or voters, helped achieve government policy goals, improved public safety, or tackled broader societal ills, such as homelessness."[30]

In other words, all those he'd referred to earlier as "not driven by a financial return...."

Here's the "proof"

This decision was made when purpose madness was peaking at Cannes and D&AD. In the IPA's case, one imagines that its leaders justified misplacing their marbles by citing research done by Peter Field - author of many of the IPA's most influential reports.

Often referred to as the "guru of effectiveness", Field had used the IPA's Effworks Global Conference to unveil his latest analysis of the IPA Awards Data Bank. As he explained: "As we see here, there can be considerable benefits for companies in deploying brand purpose campaigns – both for engaging their own employees, stakeholders and investors as well as for driving customer sales. When it is done well, when it is genuine and credible, brand purpose can be very powerful."[31]

And he went on to prove that by showing the results of purpose and non-purpose campaigns - with the former leading the way on such metrics as customer acquisition, market share growth and brand appeal.

This led Janet Hull OBE, IPA director of marketing strategy and executive director IPA EffWorks to conclude "Even though brand purpose is a relatively new science, there is already evidence coming from the IPA Databank of the range of its appeal to different stakeholders. Given growing industry interest in brand purpose strategies we can expect to see many more cases in the 2022 IPA Effectiveness Awards to take our learning forward."[32]

She neglected to add - "especially if we doctor the entry requirements for them."

Questioning the research

After the initial interest in Peter Field's findings, some started to question the methodology. And critics like Richard Shotton and Mark Ritson pointed out that Field had been selective in his choice of campaigns.

He had, as Shotton observed, focused on "a subset of purpose ads – the well-executed ones [versus] all non-purposeful ads" which skewed any conclusions in favour of purpose. However, when the IPA database's purpose campaigns were assessed in their entirety, they had performed notably worse than those that focused on selling on the merits of the product or service alone."[33]

Then, a little later, Nick Asbury dug into who had sponsored the Field's research and found it to be Danone.[34]

At the time, the person who was running Danone's marketing, Valerie Hernando-Presse was so woke, she made her counterpart at Unilever, Aline Santos, look like a Victorian mill owner.

Prone to observations like: "In this people-powered world, the way we've done marketing - selling more stuff to more people - is over ... We want all our brands to put purpose at the center and commit to this food revolution."

That was back in 2019 when that kind of talk was the stuff of the conference circuit.

But, by the time Peter Field was doing the research for Danone, its share price and sales were tanking, Danone had recently laid off 2,000 people and CEO Emmanuel Faber - the purpose and ESG advocate - had just been fired.

Reality had dawned on the shareholders at Danone. And Hernando-Presse desperately needed some good news to stop her following Faber out the door.

Suffice to say, she did exactly that last year. And Danone's marketing has reverted to a more traditional approach.

The same belatedly might be said of the IPA.

"For goodness sake, let's have some fun"

Its *volte-face* hasn't been as remarkable as the D&AD's. However it, too, seems to have realised that purpose has had its day and, in BBH's Karen Martin, has appointed a president who wants to get back to basics.

She set out her stall early saying, "Creativity isn't a nice to have. It's all we have. Let's protect it and put it back at the heart of everything we do. And for goodness sake, let's have some fun."[35]

One might hope that her sign off is a response to the hyperseriousness that characterised the purpose decade.

That may be so, but whoever wrote the IPA bio of their new president was keen to remind us "Karen Martin is one of the industry's most progressive and dynamic leaders."[36]

Oh dear.

Will the activists, careerists and those who reflexively repeat the mantras ever give up the fight? I doubt it. They have convinced themselves there is only one truth, of which they are the arbiter. Which renders them incapable of doubt and critical thinking.

Is that too damning? Well, let's stick with the IPA for a couple of minutes more, should we?

The non-debate

Last October, they organised a debate at the Palace of Westminster with the initially encouraging title: "The Anti-Woke Agenda is Fuelling Creativity".[37]

On stage were Paul Bainsfair the director general of the IPA, Stephen Woodford, CEO of the Advertising Association, the strategist, Lucy Barbour, another strategist cum diversity advocate, Asad Dhunna, writer Shelina Janmohamed and the CCO at Ogilvy, Andre (Dede) Laurentino.

The evening kicked off with Assad Dhunna explaining that the term "woke" is not new. And how its etymology can be traced to those resisting the horrific orgy of lynchings that terrorised the black population in the American Deep South as recently as the 1930s.

It was a masterful debating ploy, likely to give pause to anyone who entered the room with any "anti-woke" sentiments.

But what made it more remarkable was the fact that the speaker was supposed to be arguing "For" the "anti-woke agenda." And it set the tone for the "debate" itself, during which all four participants argued against the motion!

Take a look at The Debating Group's analysis of the "discussion" and how the participants banged on in mutual agreement, incapable of seeing the absurdity of their unanimity.[38] To them, woke represented all that was right and good. As for anti-woke, they might well have been discussing the anti-Christ.

Another snow job

There was no mention of the widely held view that woke's belief system is synonymous with cancellation, de-platforming, trigger warnings and the danger of misspeaking. Or that, in "unconscious bias", it asserts that all white people are inevitably racist whether they realise it or not. Thus automatically calling into question any opinion they might be bold enough to offer.

No one referenced the above - or the idea that such traits might just be inimical to the expression of alternate points of view, original thinking or creativity.

On the contrary, the speakers inveighed against a diabolical "anti-woke movement". I attended with Nick Asbury and we tried our best to see our creative industry in this context. Eventually we had to explain that, at that time, the "anti-woke movement" in UK advertising essentially amounted to him and me.

I also pointed out that in our world, woke (in the form of social purpose campaigns) had not been undermined by some fiendish cabal (i.e. Nick and me), it had been rejected by a) our clients and b) the consuming general public.

Aside from that, there was no mention (never mind critique) of woke censoriousness (and groupthink) and its baleful impact on creativity.

Which surely is what we should've been debating.

But then again, it's a discussion that our industry leaders had been avoiding for many years, and they probably went home happy at another snow job well done.

The party line

The aim was to avoid any debate, and to keep the conversation focused on the party line. And for years that applied across all our institutions.

I remember being delighted to see the eminently sensible and very business-like Dame Annette King installed as the chair of the Advertising Association. But my heart sank when she told us all that: "The AA is an impressive organisation with an agenda to drive change. The work the AA is doing on diversity and inclusion and climate change, and in other important areas, is very close to my heart and something I'm committed to accelerating."[39]

In other words, the same progressive gaze and consequent blindness to advertising's main problems. Namely: clients don't see its value ... the public ignores or blocks it ... and most of the people who work in it are deeply unhappy.

As D&AD's Tim Lindsay had observed at much the same time as Annette's elevation: "Where once the public rather liked advertising and we liked working in the business, our consuming public now do pretty much anything to avoid it, and sadly a lot of us are looking for ways to leave."[40]

As we'll see in more detail in Part 2, Tim and other leaders of the industry's institutions have had no success in rectifying this. Like Annette they've focused instead upon, yes, "the agenda to drive change ... on diversity and inclusion and climate change".

Avoiding reality

It wasn't just issues that were being avoided. Often, it was reality.

Take, for example, this from the 2024 Salary Survey report by Major Players, the advertising industry's biggest recruitment company.

At that time, it was plain to see that the wheels had come off the purpose bandwagon. Yet the editors of the report were determined to get out and give it this push:

"Businesses are placing far greater emphasis on purpose and ESG, with nine in ten decision-makers classifying these aspects of governance as a priority in their strategic plans. This reflects a paradigm shift in how companies are viewing themselves and the responsibilities they have to society ... Businesses that harness change and establish purpose at the core of their business can engage and retain employees more successfully, and can be much more innovative and transformative."[41]

Whoever wrote and approved that was blind to what had happened in the industry. And also to the reality writ large in their own survey's data.

Respondents - aged from 18 to over 55 - were asked to list the reasons they chose a job. Across the 14 disciplines questioned - from "Client Service" to "UX - User Experience" - commitment to social purpose or ethical behaviour/environmental impact did not get a single mention.

The answers were:

For permanent staff:
1) Salary and Bonus
2) Good work life balance
3) Positive Environment
4) Interesting Projects
5) Culture

And similarly for freelancers:
1) Day rate
2) Good work life balance
3) Flexibility/remote working
4) Positive environment
5) Interesting projects[42]

In common with most aspects of life, self-interest (salary/day rate) trumped altruism (purpose).

And, as we've seen, that same basic instinct has reasserted itself across adland.

The cost of living crisis, supply chain disruption, inflation and high interest rates had awakened clients and their CMOs to commercial reality. And their agencies had to follow.

But in some cases, begrudgingly. For there are those who still cling to their commitment to social purpose. The hardliners realise they must endure the resurgence of commercial purpose. And wait for the pendulum to swing back to work that serves their progressive agenda.

However, while this means they have lost control of adland's output, they've tried to tighten their grip on the everyday agency life.

Indeed, instead of politicising the work, they're turned their attention to the workplace. And here the moral high ground upon which they've built their stronghold is Diversity, Equity and Inclusion (DE+I).

Let's see if it's a redoubt from which to launch a counter-offensive or the place where they'll be making their last stand.

7
Equity or enmity?

We've just seen how our institutions encouraged the activists and careerists to use their ads to change the world. Industry leaders have been equally complicit when it comes to transforming the workplace through DE+I

In fact, senior management have indirectly been the driving force of this transition.

I say, "indirectly" because they've done it at arm's length by signing off the ever-expanding remit of HR - and empowering a very willing army of back office bureaucrats to make it happen.

This, it must be stressed, is not an advertising phenomenon.

Assessing the period 2011 - 2023, the British Labour Force Survey (LFS) shows an 83% increase in the number of people employed in HR - from just under 300,000 to more than 500,000.[1]

As a result, the sector now makes up 1.6% of all occupations in the UK.[2] Which means we have the second largest HR sector in the world. And it will be expanding on steroids once the Labour government brings into law its Employment Rights Bill.

The emphasis will then be on ensuring that those rights are entrenched and enforced. And that will require ever more HR professionals to help keep management out of the courts and tribunals.

It was not always like this.

The growth of HR

Initially the purpose of personnel management was simple: to increase competitiveness and productivity through recruitment, training and compliance with processes that achieved greater efficiency.

However, the growth of social democratic welfarism in the post-war period saw a gradual shift from management's priorities towards workers' rights. This was accelerated by rafts of legislation. And by the emergence of a professional cadre who could negotiate the legal labyrinth that was being created.

Then, as Pamela Dow, the former executive director of the Cabinet Office points out: "A further shift towards employee well-being, and diversity, equality and inclusion (DEI), in the last 20 years has completed HR's evolution from responding to business needs, to shaping them."[3]

All of which means that, as well as being highly influential, HR is now a very well paid job. In fact, in the past 12 months alone, the median salary for HR directors has increased by 20.9 per cent – from £111,982 to £135,381.[4]

The role also comes with power and prestige. Even back in 2017 KPMG found that 70% of FTSE100 companies had a chief HR or people officer on their executive committee.[5] The figure will be much higher today.

With a seat at the big table, HR's leaders will inevitably fight their corner when it comes to budget allocation. Especially as more legislation makes the workload bigger, the job more complex and their involvement more necessary.

What's wrong with ERGs

That's already happened in adland. At one network agency I visited earlier this year, the number of HR staff had increased from 3 in 2019 to twelve. That included six who were looking after "Talent". A large part of their remit involved recruitment. Which, as we're about to see, is a responsibility fraught with the potential for abuse.

Another six looked after employees i.e. each having a portfolio of client accounts which they supported with everything from maternity leave to redundancy and dismissal. Then, in addition to these, were the people dedicated to DE+I.

One of their key tasks was to distribute power to and work with the employee resource groups (ERGs) - the internal communities that represent the agency's minorities i.e. the female, black, neurodiverse and LGBTQ+ members of staff.

These special interest groups are there to help HR on policy creation as it pertains to their members. With their own budgets and allocated time resources they also organise mentorship/retention programmes plus social and training events on subjects like sexism, unconscious bias, white privilege and the other grievances that their members might harbour.[6]

In effect, ERGs divide the workplace into factions based upon identity - and a never-far-from-the-surface sense of victimhood.

Which isn't exactly helpful if you're trying to establish a unifying corporate/work culture. By accentuating the differences within the organisation, you serve to heighten the perception of each group's separateness and weaken any sense of shared mission and *esprit de coeur.*

Old school Left-wing critics are adamant that that also applies if you are trying to build solidarity amongst the workforce. As communist commentator Ash Sarkar has said about the divisions caused by conflicting identities, "we are not comrades but competitors in the mad scramble for recognition."[7]

Which is a crucial point we'll return to later.

The allure of DE+I

As this identitarian division of the workplace has spread through UK business, DE+I departments have thrived. Research cited in the independent Inclusion at

Work Panel report published in March 2024 found that the UK employs almost twice as many DE+I workers (per 10,000 employees) as any other country.[8]

There's no shortage of recruits for these jobs. And no wonder.

Our universities are churning out more graduates than our economy needs.[9] This has left us with a surplus of elites struggling to find a niche in the brickwork of a capitalist system that many have been taught to loathe.

Which brings us to another of DE+I's appeals. Aside from a good salary, power and status, the role has political influence.

And why should that be important?

Well, it's unlikely that many science, technology, engineering and mathematics graduates will be attracted to HR or DE+I. Instead, the majority come from humanities, arts and social sciences. And, while they may have picked up a worthless degree, they will also have been schooled in the ideology that dominates academia in both the US and the UK.

Critical Social Justice

To understand why proponents of Critical Social Justice are such dangerous cuckoos to invite into adland's nest, let's look at the foundational beliefs they'll be bringing into your agency.

We'll start with the view, propounded by such postmodernists as Michel Foucault, Jacques Derrida and Jean-François Lyotard, that none of us - regardless of race, ethnicity or sexuality - can understand reality.

Modern science, reason and what we think of as democratic ideals are also a sham. Even language, as Derrida saw it, is a tool for maintaining the status quo - and cannot be trusted.[10]

Critical Race Theorists like Derrick Bell, Kimberle Crenshaw and Judith Butler have adapted these tenets and identified exactly who that status quo benefits and who it oppresses.

They and the ideologues who've succeeded them have concluded: a) our "reality" is simply a false consciousness designed to perpetuate the power of the white Patriarchy b) That power structure can best be dismantled by the pursuit of equity c) This is achieved by redistributing resources (in adland's terms: salaries, jobs, promotions, bonuses etc) on the basis of identity d) Which entails penalising the individual white person for ongoing wrongs and also those perpetrated by white people generations ago.[11]

In short, the white, heterosexual male stands atop the pyramid of oppression. Beneath him are differing levels of oppressor and oppressed. So a white, heterosexual woman is dominated by her male counterpart. But she'll have been simultaneously dumping on everyone else.

Regarding "everyone else", their place in the hierarchy is worked out on the basis of gender, race, sexuality, disability or other persecuted characteristics.[12]

The meaning of equity

As noted above, equity is the means of getting justice for the oppressed. This is usually explained as the rejection of equality of opportunity in favour of equality of outcomes.

While that might appear to be a slight semantic shift, the implications are profound. For it replaces the notion that you might prosper as a result of your merits with a new belief in advancement determined by your identity.

And, in the grievance culture fostered by these identity politics, it pays to find a place as high up the pyramid of oppression as possible.

We've borrowed this belief system direct from the US, so given that country's history of enslavement and racial discrimination, the best card to play is a black one. But it is possible to trump that by claiming the intersection of a racial characteristic with, say, a disability or perhaps membership of the LGBTQ+ community. Having all three is a truly winning hand.

As Labour activist Ben Cobley points out in his seminal work *The Tribe: The Liberal Left and the System of Diversity*: "The creation of favoured and unfavoured group categories directs favour and protection towards one set of groups, (the non-white, the female, the homosexual, the Muslim, immigrants) but not the other set (the white, the male, the heterosexual, Christian, ethnic British and especially English.) Favoured groups receive protection against criticism and other negativity but unfavoured groups receive no such protection leaving them open to disparagement and generalised disfavour in the public sphere."[13]

In other words it generates a toxic atmosphere of mutual resentment in which there's little point in trying to empathise with those who do not share your racial/gender/physical attributes. All you can do is participate in the zero sum battle for power between your group and the opposing identities.

Ibram X. Kendi spells out the mutual hostility in *How to be an Antiracist*: "The only remedy to racist discrimination is antiracist discrimination. The only remedy to past discrimination is present discrimination. The only remedy to present discrimination is future discrimination."[14]

As we saw on pages 33-36, the ideology for which Kendi speaks is baked into university departments of humanities, arts and social sciences. You'd hope, however, that those who teach and study marketing and advertising courses might be less political and more pragmatic.

Unfortunately not.

One tutor's experience

Gail Parminter is a copywriter who's worked at great shops like Ogilvy & Mather and Saatchi & Saatchi. She has also taught at some of the industry's most prestigious colleges. Here are her recollections of life at the chalkface:

"Not all, but some of those places were in thrall to Critical Race Theory and BLM. While most of the tutors were not " woke", we were all conscious of the danger of the threat of cancellation if we questioned either or voiced another point of view. Likewise gender ideology and queer theory were a given. Actually it was all about trans rights while the LGB factions were practically ignored.

"The 'student voice' was king. They were actively encouraged to complain and report staff who they perceived to be not woke or not woke enough. I was accused of everything from racial discrimination to being a TERF [Trans Exclusionary Radical Feminist].

"Ableism was also high on the agenda with disabilities, especially 'hidden' ones. These were prioritised and staff asked to endlessly accommodate their "needs". For example, marking had to be adjusted if any of the students had any physical or mental disability. A student who had the slightest bit of (usually self-diagnosed) anxiety or depression had their condition factored into the marking of their work, and was dealt with leniently when it came to non-attendance.

"Some students would not attend for weeks claiming some sort of, again self - diagnosed, issue. And tutors would then have to give extra tutorials to help them catch up. Not that some of them bothered about being behind. Some overseas students were only there for the visa that allowed them to stay in the UK for two years after graduating. They rarely attended but fully expected to be given pass marks at the end of the course.

"We were told to increase the number of BAME students. And were informed we had to "decolonise" the curriculum. So this meant ignoring books by "straight white" authors. Likewise we had to limit the number of white visiting lecturers and try to find those of a more "diverse" background.

"Even students who arrived apolitical and tried to avoid the student politics would have found it difficult to emerge unaffected by Critical Theory."[15]

Advertising veteran, Dave Trott, has observed how this plays out in agency life: "At university, we learn our purpose is to educate the world to a woke agenda. It's a noble quest and anything else is ignorant and stupid. We bring this into advertising and believe that is the whole purpose of our job ... Believing that every right-thinking person must think exactly like us. Those who don't think like us are wrong and therefore not worth considering. They can safely be ignored."[16]

Those who are, themselves, ardent supporters of diversity have explained why bringing this "woke agenda" into work might not be a great idea.

Bending the law to suit themselves

Baroness Morrissey, the City veteran who founded the 30pc Club that led a global crusade for more female representation in the boardroom recently wrote on social media: "The DEI 'industry' is partly to blame for the present situation as some of the efforts and language have (ironically) been exclusionary favouring certain groups over others, discouraging diverse viewpoints or prioritising identity factors over merit rather than creating opportunity for all...."[17]

If you listen to Tanya de Grunwald's revelatory podcasts "This Isn't Working" you'll hear a steady stream of leading HR practitioners who endorse this assessment.

For example, Neil Morrison, HR Director at Severn Trent and Levi Pay formerly of Stonewall and the Commission for Racial Equality say there's little understanding of the Equality Act of 2010.

Morrison suggests that less than 10% of DE+I operatives understand it. Levi Pay reckons it is worse than that. He can count the DE+I practitioners who can give "a really cogent explanation for the concepts and boundaries of the legislation" on the fingers of one hand.[18]

Both agree that activists apply their own hierarchy of protected characteristics to the detriment of other employees' interests. In short, they interpret - and break - the law to suit themselves. And turn positive discrimination into pay and hiring policy.

Favouring some identities over others

Every week throws up new examples of how this affects our largest institutions. Figures show that the BBC's senior LGBT managers earn a median average of 15.6% more than heterosexuals. And senior managers from BAME backgrounds earn a median average 12.6% more than white ones.[19]

A few days after the BBC revelations, came the publication of a report on diversity in the outgoing Scottish National Party Government. It showed that lesbian, gay and bisexual staff were almost 50% more likely to be given a "substantive" promotion than straight colleagues.[20]

In both cases, it seems that implementing equity has led to certain identities being favoured over others. And the very thing that it is supposed to be eliminating, i.e. discrimination, is being promoted.

Could it be that we've also adopted the same kind of discriminatory practices here in adland? And do we, to borrow Ben Cobley's distinction, have our own "favoured" and "unfavoured" groups?

Well, one London-based creative director who's responsible for a multinational account, told me that if he chooses a BAME candidate for a job, his judgement is accepted without question. But if he opts for a white, male candidate he must provide a rationale for his choice.[21]

This apparently is not uncommon practice across the industry.

If that's so, then the rationale lies in the targets that have been set to achieve the "requisite" levels of diversity.

The target setter in chief has been the Institute of Practitioners in Advertising. It was back in 2016 that its president, Tom Knox, announced that the industry must aim for 40% of senior positions to be held by women and at least 15% of leadership positions to be held by non-white personnel.

Additionally, 25% of new hires were to be from BAME backgrounds.[22]

Targets, I hasten to add, are not official quotas. And therefore hitting them is left to the discretion of the management of individual agencies.

That's the theory anyway. But the progressive groupthink won't tolerate too much in the way of deviation.

The pressure is on to hit the hiring targets

Take, for example, the pressure exerted by the *Campaign* School Reports.[23]

In this, our trade magazine's flagship feature, the editorial staff score each agency points out of 10 for the past year's performance.

Prior to its publication, around 100 of the UK's leading shops are asked to complete a detailed review of their previous 12 months performance: listing their increase/decrease in headcount, accounts lost and gained plus other information like major hirings and awards won.

So far, so commercial.

But the agencies are also allowed the opportunity to score points for being good progressive citizens. So it does them no harm to cite the social purpose and cause-related work they have done. And to reference their commitment to what the editors of *Campaign* regard as social responsibility.

Then, crucially, they are asked to explain how they've been promoting diversity and inclusion within their teams. And, of course, these are based not on measurements of much needed cognitive diversity or socio-economic diversity but on the identitarian criteria of gender and ethnicity.

Failure to provide this information earns this reprimand on their School Report:

"This is a provisional score as the agency has not provided sufficient diversity information."

So as an agency you have to buy into the target system and, therefore, the identitarian ideology from which it proceeds.

And, one suspects, those who don't measure up to the *Campaign* staff's progressive standards are marked down.

Which means you could have retained all your clients, picked up five huge pieces of business and won a ton of metal in the past 12 months, but if your agency's business objectives and achievements - and your politics - aren't aligned with those of the progressive groupthink, you're not going to get the full recognition you deserve.

Innately competitive agency heads know the School Reports are pored over by clients, potential new hires and rivals. And they're aware they will be judged by the score they receive. So they play the game, and the fixation with identity politics goes unchallenged. As does the tacit encouragement of affirmative action and the inevitable side effect of discrimination against unfavoured groups.

That's troubling enough. But when the task of hiring is left in the hands of politicised personnel, the problem in adland runs even deeper.

Let's begin with the efforts to increase the number - and paypackets - of women in advertising.

8
Positive discrimination in adland?

On the face of it, there's a glaring inequality in the gap between what men and women are paid.

According to *Campaign's* latest analysis of yearly government data, it is 9.79%.[1]

We're talking here of the aggregate earnings of men versus the aggregate earnings of women. And there's one fairly obvious cause for the gap. There still aren't enough women pulling in the big salaries at the very top of the industry.

According to the IPA Census for 2025, women occupy 46% of C-suite roles.[2]

Which means that, while advances are being made, there are still not enough women making the leap into the six figure salary bracket.

Why is that? Well, according to Richard Reeves, social scientist and senior fellow at The Brookings Institution, the "one word explanation" is "children."

He has found that among young childless adults, the pay gap has essentially disappeared. Marianne Bertrand adds: "There's remarkable evidence that earnings for men and women move in sync up until the birth of a couple's first child."[3]

Which is bad news for advertising's gifted and ambitious women. The average age of the UK's richer first time mothers is roughly equivalent to that at which they become candidates for a place on the board.

Alas, after that, as Henrik Kleven found in reviewing wage gap data from 134 countries, "In general, women don't recover. They don't catch back up to men, even many years after first childbirth."[4]

A lack of supply and not demand

There are several reasons for this career derailment. The most obvious being men failing to do their share of the child caring, inflexible work regimes and a lack of affordable childcare.

There's also the simple fact that some women find caring for the baby they've been carrying for nine months a more appealing option than managing the team they probably carry week in, week out.

We might also take into account the influence of homogamy. This is the growing tendency for well-off people, like the adlanders who are rising through the ranks, to marry horizontally i.e. to another well-off person.

It was French sociologist Pierre Bourdieu who explained: "When two privileged individuals marry, they not only mutually affirm their classed ways of being, they also create a highly privileged family through which resources can be combined. Joining forces consolidates privileges and advantages for the individuals involved (and their children) and it can intensify class divisions more generally."[5]

One of those privileges/advantages is being able to afford to quit work for a few years to raise the kids, or to return to work part-time or in less pressured and, consequently, lower paid roles.

So, with all this in mind, it's worth considering that the shortage of women at C-level may be due not to a discriminatory lack of demand. The problem might be a lack of supply.

It could be that there simply aren't enough qualified candidates on the market.

Aiming for 50/50 parity at CEO level

It's unlikely this theory has much traction within the industry body that's pushing for pay parity at the highest level. As the name suggests, Women in Advertising and Communication Leadership (WACL) is highly focussed on promoting the interests of women at the upper end of the pay grades.

As such, after hitting the IPA's target of 40% representation in senior positions, in April 2023, WACL launched its campaign calling for a 50/50 gender split among chief executive roles across the industry.[6]

It had an immediate effect. According to *Campaign* School Reports data, covering the 12 months up to the end of 2023, 31.3% of the 99 agencies polled had a CEO who had been in their role for one year or less. And notably, among those 31 leaders, 17 were women.[7]

Since then there has been a scramble to get the best women into adland's boardrooms. Which means the gifted have been in very high demand for the very top posts. And some of the lesser qualified have ridden on their skirt tails.

Nevertheless, the destination of 50/50 remains a few years ahead and the big bump in the road to parity remains motherhood.

Progressives, however, prefer to see the continued disparity as a consequence of sexual discrimination at the hands of the Patriarchy.

Given that the vast majority of the women striving for 50/50 CEO parity are white and from relatively privileged backgrounds, this claim to victimhood is useful. Because it means they can escape the obloquy heaped upon their white male counterparts, and even qualify for the favoured status that accrues to members of an oppressed group.

Few people in adland would dare to openly question the view that being in the oppressed group has held women back. However, one such individual is writer Paul Burke. And he has stood this argument on its head and identified favoured status as the unforeseen cause of the gender pay gap.[8]

Women on top

As I'm sure Paul would tell you, the overall picture of women in the UK workplace is actually promising.

They appear to be winning the war for workplace domination. Much to the chagrin of those who see themselves on the losing side.

According to Channel 4 research "Trends, Truth and Trust", nearly half of Gen Z men (45%) believe that "we have gone so far in promoting women's equality that we are discriminating against men".[9]

Recent salary statistics suggest why they think this way. According to the Centre for Social Justice, for people in their age group, the gender pay gap has been reversed. In 2020-21, the average annual salary for a young man was £24,032, compared to £23,021 for a young woman. By 2022-23, male wages had stagnated at £24,283, while female earnings had risen to £26,476 - a 9% difference.[10]

There are no figures regarding pay discrepancy in this salary band in advertising. But what is clear is that females are being recruited in greater numbers than male candidates.

According to the most recent IPA figures, men account for 40% of the total employed base while females account for 60%. And this gap is widening year-on-year.[11]

Last year, over two thirds of staff at Elvis, Dentsu Creative and MullenLowe London were women, with BBH (65%) and New Commercial Arts (64%) not far behind.[12]

A sizeable majority of the lower-paid, first-rung opportunities in our industry, once given to young men, now go to their female counterparts. Not just junior creative positions but entry-level roles in account management, planning, production and across the digital disciplines.

As the 2024 IPA Agency Census tells us, in the creative agencies, 64% of all apprentices/graduates and 62.5% of junior executives are women.[13]

"It's like Mad Men but with way more Peggys"

The over-representation of young, female talent is reflected in *Campaign* "Faces to Watch". For 2022 the female/male ratio was 21:12; for 2023 it was 24:10 and for 2024 it was 23:9.[14]

Aside from the possibility that *Campaign* is biased in its choice of up-and-coming stars, this would suggest that the young women entering our industry are more than twice as bright as their male counterparts. The other, more realistic, explanation is that young women are being given preferential treatment at recruitment stage - and there are simply more of them for *Campaign* to choose from.

In the article accompanying the most recent "Faces...", We Are Social's senior creative, Polly Norkett, said that the best way to recruit youngsters into the industry was to: "Tell them it's like *Mad Men* but with way more Peggys."[15]

She wasn't kidding.

The "Faces to Watch" are *Campaigns* top tips for the next generation of agency stars. But what about those who've already made it?

Here the picture for women' s representation is also encouraging. Indeed, they are far exceeding the IPA's target of 40% of senior roles.

According to *Campaign*'s most recent "School Report" data the industry figure stands at 50.4%.

At Publicis London, 77% of senior management roles are held by women. At Saatchi & Saatchi, the UK's largest agency, it's 71%. At MullenLowe it's 69%, at VML and Iris it's 64%, which is the same percentage as leading independent shop, Wonderhood Studios.[16]

In fact, across the big agencies, women dominate in many of the senior roles with 64.5% of heads of account management/client services; 55.2% business directors; 54.3% of heads of new business/new business director; 52.3% of other senior staff and 58.1% of all managers.[17]

Sisters are doin' it for themselves

If women outnumber men in these senior roles, why is the gender pay gap still at 9%? Well, as we discussed earlier, the lack of C-Level representation is still a contributing factor.

But, according to Paul Burke, the main problem lies not at the top of the pay scale but at the bottom.

As we've seen, females are now flooding in at the trainee and new recruit level. And if the gender pay gap is, indeed, the difference between the aggregate earnings of men and women throughout the business then it is these ranks of lowly paid recent entrants that are dragging down the women's overall salary stats.

Paul maintains, therefore, that the perpetuation of the gender pay gap is a result of not so much the discrimination against women but the bias towards hiring females and the subsequent over-representation in the lower echelons.

And I would suggest that that's because those doing the hiring are bringing their own perspective to the job and recruiting in their own image. A case of sub-conscious bias, perhaps? Moreover, in the name of equity, they are favouring the protected identity with whom they most relate at the expense of other candidates.

If you think that thesis is far-fetched, remember the experts' conclusion that only a handful of HR/DE+I executives understand the Equality Act, and that many abuse their power and discriminate.

Again, too far fetched? Well, you might be interested to know that there's one department in adland that's characterised by a massive gender imbalance.

When it comes to Chief HR Officer/Chief People Officer/Head of HR/HR Director some 81% are women. Likewise 84% of all HR staff.[18]

LGBTQ+? Doing OK

Given the above statistic, it would be interesting to know how many LGBTQ+ people are drawn to HR and the people-management of agency life.

Because we also see evidence of over-indexing in employment of this favoured identity. For how else would you explain that in 2023, people "identifying with being asexual, bisexual, demisexual, gay, pansexual, queer, or other", made up 18% of the creative industries' workforce?[19]

Or how, according to the 2025 Major Players Salary Survey, 18.3% of the most prestigious roles - those in client service and strategy, creative service, creative, design and studio - are accounted for by LGBTQIA+ personnel?[20]

In the digital disciplines, perhaps the most important - social, content and influencer - the figure is 22%.[21]

Last year's survey by the same much respected organisation, revealed that 18% of senior leadership and C-suite positions - with salaries over £70,000 pa - were held by individuals identifying as LGBTQIA+.[22]

The latest IPA All in Census says the overall figure is more like 12% and puts C-Level representation at 10%. All of whom spring from the 3% of the UK population who, according to the IPA, identify as LGBQ+.[23]

Now, given the age profile of the advertising industry, we should take into account the differences of those self-identifying as LBGTQ+ that exist across age groups. And that the young are more gender/sexually fluid.

But if we just focus on the industry's 16-34 year olds that's still only 8.2% of the population.[24] So there's a hiring imbalance here that is hard to explain without concluding there's a bias toward LGBTQIA+ recruits.

Answer these two questions

Incidentally, the most recent UK Census indicated that the four most popular jobs amongst gay and bi-sexual individuals were "coffee shop workers" (10.8%) then "leisure/theme park attendants" (11%) followed by "actors/entertainers/presenters" (12.3%). Eclipsing all these was "airline cabin crew" at 13.7%.[25]

But, it seems they got that wrong. Because working in adland now appears to be *the* job of choice for members of the LGBTQIA+ community.

Either that or could we just be discriminating in their favour when it comes to recruitment? And if that's the case, it might be wise to ask a couple of questions:

#1: Are these new recruits hired because they best understand the general public that adland so desperately needs to re-engage? If so, what special insight does this discrete cohort possess that other recruits do not?

#2: Are they being taken on because they belong to an historically under-represented group? If that's the case then is compensatory hiring going to correct the disconnect between adland's elite and the mass of people who live beyond their bubble?

Or is this an example of DE+I overreach that's resulted in the deliberate over-representation of one identity group to the detriment of other candidates? If so then perhaps we should also be asking if shrinking the talent pool in this way has impaired agencies' ability to serve their clients as best they might?

42% of new entrants are BAME

The same questions could be asked when it comes to hiring on the basis of race and ethnic background.

According to the *Campaign* "School Report" for 2025, some 42.8% of new entrants in advertising were from an ethnic minority background.[26]

If one of equity's main objectives is to level up employment to match that of the BAME representation in the general UK population, that's 42.8% as opposed to 18%.[27]

You might argue that adland's London-based agencies are simply recruiting to match the capital's profile, where the % of BAME people is much closer to 42%.[28]

But if that's true then why, when our audience is national, are we seeking only to reflect what is happening in London?

It's a common complaint that adland rarely hires anyone from north of the Tottenham Hotspur Stadium. So why would you take London as your template for demographic balance? Surely you would just be compounding the "London Bubble" effect.

The other reason might be that agencies are just too eager to hit the IPA's target of 25% of new recruits to the industry coming from the non-white community.

Why the IPA's BAME targets may not be a great idea

If that's the case then setting and wildly exceeding targets like this might not be doing BAME candidates too many favours. They give unsuitable white male candidates a convenient excuse for why they failed to be hired - and a divisive, lasting feeling of resentment.

Simultaneously, they can unfairly cast doubts about the suitability of BAME candidates who succeed on merit. It has been suggested that people from a BAME background are already more susceptible to Imposter Syndrome. The suspicion that you're a "diversity hire" can only accentuate such insecurity.[29]

While we're speaking of insecurity, encouraging marginalised groups to see themselves as permanent victims is, itself, disempowering - not to mention demeaning. For it simultaneously stokes a sense of grievance whilst encouraging them to expect some benevolent and paternalistic institution (the DI+E department) to act as their saviour.

It might also be worth questioning if the emphasis on colour is the best way of achieving the cognitive diversity that the industry so desperately lacks? What happens if hitting targets simply results in a new influx of middle class people (remember, at the last count, fully 69% of BAME adlanders were privately educated)?[30]

Surely this is the inevitable consequence of having race and identity as the criteria behind your diversity drive. For it allows clued-up members of the favoured minorities to game the system.

After all, if the recruiting organisation has boxes that need to be ticked, it will be difficult competing for a job against someone who starts their interview: "As an Asian, gay man in advertising…" even when that person is the university-educated son of posh parents who live in Chiswick.

The downside of all this was explained by an independent panel of DE+I experts when reporting to the government in 2024: "An organisation may be proportionately representative of the population in gender and race. However, if the workforce remains by and large socio-economically and also geographi-cally homogenous (for example, composed of middle-class graduates from South East England) it is likely unrepresentative in life experience and values."[31]

It was a point amplified by equitable workplace activist Aparna Rae when writing in *Forbes* magazine:

"The reality is that DEI has functioned as a privilege multiplier, benefiting those already in relatively secure professional roles while leaving behind the very people it claims to serve."[32]

What about class?

Speaking of the left behind, might some consideration be given to the idea that class is *the* crucial determinant? And that the DE+I affirmative action initiatives do nothing for - indeed discriminate against - those who make up the largest self-identifying cohort in UK society: the working class?

Let me emphasise that focussing on the 56% of the UK population who identify as working class would not staunch the flow of what the IPA terms non-white people entering the industry.[33] Our BAME citizens are disproportionately found in the C2DE classification. So a focus on working class recruitment should give us a workforce that more than matches the BAME share of the general population.

Likewise it would bring in working class recruits from the LGBTQ+, women and all other minorities communities. And it would inject a massive infusion of majority beliefs and values, opinions and lived experiences that are currently unrepresented in London's agencies.

But, according to the IPA All in Census for 2025, the number of working class people in the industry has actually declined. They now make up just 19% of adland's workforce. In contrast, almost the same percentage of people (18%) in the industry attended a fee-paying school.

Dan Wilks, director of the advertising industry think tank Credos, explained: "People from a working class background are the most under-represented in our industry. If we are serious about representation, we must address this."[34]

But that's unlikely to happen. Adland's Left-leaning progressives aren't interested in the working class - or elevating their social or economic status. Moreover, they are particularly unsympathetic towards the white working class.

As we've noted, they have adopted the idea that prejudice against minority groups, and not class privilege, is the country's most significant dividing line. And, like their US counterparts, they see everything through Critical Theory's prism of race, ethnicity, gender and sexual preference.

So, according to their dogma, those Caucasians who actually languish at the lowest level of the social scale are, by accident of birth, privileged. And all sympathy, support and advantage must go to those beneath them in the progressive's hierarchy of oppression.

We've just seen how this is affecting who comes into the industry - and who is denied access.

Its most obvious impact, however, is apparent in who actually appears in the advertising we're producing. Because the fixation with equity for the black community has pushed white working class and South and East Asian faces off our screens.

9
Why there are so many (not very) black faces on your screens

This bias began in earnest back on May 25th, 2020 with the murder of George Floyd by members of the Minneapolis Police Department.[1]

Like most UK industries and institutions, adland was caught up in the society-wide racial reckoning. We embraced the Black Lives Matter movement and took the knee. But the new and intense focus on "white privilege" and "systemic racism" also forced us to hang our heads in shame.

Because one month before Floyd's murder, the IPA published its annual Agency Census figures. And these showed that, over the previous 12 months, the already meagre number of employees of a BAME background had fallen in the workforce as a whole, and in the C-suite, too.[2]

Wherever you looked, the figures pointed to an industry that was about as diverse as your average queue at a Waitrose check out.

Black careers matter - most

Sure enough, BLM protests made the industry feel very guilty. And especially so, given the political leanings of those who work here. How embarrassing that people so influenced by Critical Social Justice should have their own racist failings highlighted.

Inevitably, in their panic, the industry fixed on the black experience - to the neglect of other minority or disadvantaged groups in society.

So, while the open letter signed by 200 agencies aimed to address "inequality and take action against racism following the death of George Floyd", its focus throughout was on the B in BAME and the need to "welcome, promote, champion, and celebrate black employees. Commit to amplifying and elevating black talent, working with black-owned businesses and supply chains."

It ended: "We, the signatories of this letter, commit to taking deep, lasting action. Today, we say George Floyd's name and stand with all black talent in our industry."

Note: "black talent." Not brown nor any other ethnic minority or disadvantaged group.

Race-washing

Confronted by the dismal lack of black people actually creating ads and running departments and agencies, adland rushed to add more DE+I specialists to its HR resources. And, as we've seen above, doubled down on the Institute of Practitioners in Advertising's target to recruit 25% of new entrants to the workforce from the non-white population.

Achieving this would, however, take too much time for a progressive industry desperate to atone for its discriminatory past.

And so, unable to swiftly redress the balance in the boardroom, adland simply projected its internal quotas into the nation's living rooms.

This was the point made by Dino Myers-Lamptey - one of the industry's most vocal proponents of a genuine response to diversity in advertising. Writing in *Campaign* he explained, "You could call this 'race washing'. Portraying inclusion and equity in advertising, yet failing to notice its deficiencies beyond the screen and take the appropriate action to deliver inclusion and equity.

"For most, the increase of black actors on screen is a step in the right direction, although for some it is like a magician's distraction from the real world action we'd all like to see."[4]

Black stereotypes

"A step in the right direction"? Actually, Dino has also argued that simply putting black faces in ads is counterproductive.

In his role as co-author of the Advertising Standards Authority's "Research into Racial & Ethnic Stereotyping in Advertising" report he noted that "portrayals of BAME people in advertising often relied on stereotypes and simplistic ideas. Examples given included Asians often being portrayed as shopkeepers or taxi drivers, and black people being shown in association with sports or music or being a joker."[5]

He's right but if stereotyping is one problem then superfluity is another with black actors now being thrown into the mix as non-speaking extras. Meanwhile, those who do have starring roles are usually cast as the middle class characters that white actors used to play.

Not too black

Either way, little effort is made to project the true black experience or the contribution the West Indian diaspora has made to life in the UK. For example, Jamaican culture is now youth culture in most of Britain's cities. However, you're unlikely to see a commercial about everyday life that reflects that.[6]

One of the riches that those with Caribbean roots have bestowed is their vibrant Pentecostal faith. The result is that some 47% of black people aged 18 to 34 are attending church at least monthly.[7] And 48% of all London's churchgoers are black.[8] But you can bet that something as conservative as churchgoing would never pass the progressive's test for inclusion in an advertising scenario.

The majority of churchgoers are now of African origin. Indeed, in the general population, they outnumber their Caribbean counterparts 2:1. Given that they've experienced less racial mixing, they are darker skinned. But you'll see very few truly black characters appearing in our ads.[9] In fact, women with lighter skin tones are four times more likely to appear in advertising than those with darker skin.[10]

This kind of superficiality is, however, still preferable to invisibility. And after years of being absent from our screens, black and mixed race viewers now seem to approve of what they are seeing.

In the September 2023 study by the Black British Voices Research Project, more than three-quarters of black British people said they believe that advertising campaigns portray black culture better than they did 10 years ago.[11]

Truth is, that's the raising of a shamefully low bar. But some much needed progress has been made. And, as a study by the advertising industry body ISBA in March 2024 indicated, 65% of all black respondents reckoned that their ethnic group was well represented in UK advertising.[12]

The invisible Asians

Unfortunately, the same satisfaction is not felt by members of other minority communities, especially those with South Asian roots. As ISBA found, only 43% of them felt that their group was well-represented.[13]

Other statistics suggest why they are unhappy.

The biggest ever study of diversity in advertising was conducted in 2019 by Channel 4 and YouGov Insight and it found that people from South Asia appeared in just 12% of ads and took the lead role in 3%. This despite the fact that they constituted 7% of the UK population.[14] At the time, that was over twice the population share of their black counterparts who, incidentally, featured in 37% of the ads and took the lead in 12% of them.[15]

That was *before* adland's BLM fixation with black participation. And the balance will have changed dramatically since then. And not in the Asians' favour.

We have no up-to-date figures for our industry. However, in TV programming, the Creative Diversity Network Report published in September 2024 noted on-screen contributions by South Asians was just 4.9%.[16]

It's unlikely that figure is any higher in advertising. As Sadia Siddiqui of the Language Matters consultancy says, "South Asians make up the second largest ethnic groups in the UK [after White British], yet we're notably absent from the British advertising landscape."[17]

If they've appeared at all then Amar Singh, head of content and communications at MKTG says, "The advertising industry in the UK has traditionally viewed British Asians as an exotic addition to a campaign, rather than having the confidence to put them at the center."[18]

Such criticism was echoed by Arif Miah and Ala Uddin, founders of Mud Orange, a creative shop aimed at redefining roles of Muslims in UK advertising. As Arif observed: "It's clear that when brands are talking to Muslims, there is a massive disconnect. They're talking to an outdated idea of Muslims who probably don't even exist anymore."[19]

Refusing to be the victim

If you think this paltry South Asian presence is bad, just consider how we treat our East Asian citizens. In the most recent ISBA study, 9% said they were happy with how they are represented in advertising.[20] It's likely they feel the same way about TV programming where they make up 0.8% of onscreen players.[21]

Given this sparse Asian representation and the near ubiquity of black faces, how do we explain this two tier approach to diversity and inclusion?

Could it be that the experience of the UK's South and East Asian immigrants doesn't fit the progressive narrative? And that their success gives the lie to Critical Race Theory and its hierarchy of oppression?

After all, if the Patriarchy is all powerful and meritocracy is a sham, how have these people of recent, often impoverished, immigrant stock been allowed to take on the white man and win?

The simple answer is by focusing on hard work, thrift, education and enterprise. In other words, by practicing the bourgeois habits of self-improvement that the Critical Theorists deride.

According to British Pakistani author, Dr Rakib Ehsan, while hard right bigots find the resulting success infuriating so, too, do "progressive activists and hard-left 'anti-racists' who increasingly treat the existence of flourishing and resilient ethnic-minority communities as an inconvenience to their pseudo-intellectual 'white privilege' theories and 'systemically racist Britain' narratives."[22]

The disappearing Jew

There is, of course, another minority group that has all but disappeared from TV's commercial breaks. I'm talking about those quintessential over-achievers, the Jews.

In the progressive gaze, their massive over-representation within the power structures of western culture and capitalism, means they're the epitome of Patriarchal privilege.

Therefore, to Critical Theorists, Jews are damned by their achievements and enjoy none of the protection the Left ostentatiously extends to the favoured minorities.

Dr Ehsan again nails it: "On the so-called 'oppression pyramid', Jews - due to their relative educational and economic success - are not viewed as a victimised group. Due to the socio economic status of particular groups, certain forms of discrimination are prioritised over others - with anti-Semitism ranking below anti-Muslim or anti-black racism."[23]

Which is why there's no one fighting the Jews' corner in adland. And why you haven't seen a Jewish character in a TV ad since Maureen Lipman's Beattie in the 1980s BT campaign.

Which brings us to another absentee from today's casting director briefs.

Just 8% are working class

That ISBA study I cited indicates that only 36% of people from the "lower social grade" feel that their group is "well represented" in UK advertising.[24]

It isn't just the ads that annoy the working classes. They're not keen on the programmes on either side of the commercial break either.

As a November 2023 Office of Communications (Ofcom) report said they see "little representation on the BBC of what they called 'normal, working class lives' … Even when they did see 'people like them' they felt the portrayal often reverted to stereotypes or 'tokenist' characterisations."[25]

That's probably because, as with advertising, there are so few working class people producing the content.

In a speech at the Edinburgh TV Festival, the UK's most eminent political playwright, James Graham, told his audience that only 8% of people in the TV industry were working class.[26]

Graham also referred to class as "everyone's least favourite diversity and representation category" and said more attention should be paid to social mobility.

The author of such dramas as *Sherwood, Dear England, Ink* and *Quiz* called for social class to be considered more often when measuring diversity within the industry.

"We are squeamish about defining it," Graham said, "and as a result, we quite often still exclude it from industry measurements around diversity."

"I could be wrong," Graham said, "but compared to other areas of under-representation, when it comes to class, I feel like we just don't feel it, as much, in our bones."[27] Perhaps what he meant was, the progressive gaze doesn't actually see it. Or want to.

"It's impossible to have any white people in a commercial"

Once more, what goes for TV goes for advertising. And again it's because the focus is on race, gender and ethnicity. The people running the diversity industry just aren't interested in the working class.

The lack of empathy - or more pertinently interest - can be seen in the ads. Outside of those for gambling sites, it is unusual to spot a member of the working class. And those tradesmen who do occasionally turn up on screen are, yes, now usually black.

It's little wonder then that September 2025's "Mirror on the Industry" report by Channel 4 showed that black actors appeared in over 50% of the top 500 adverts shown over two four-week periods.[28]

Adland's most thought-provoking observer, Rory Sutherland has commented on the imbalance: "It's one of those things that make perfect sense on an individual level. But fails collectively if and when everybody simultaneously decides that it's impossible to have any white people in a television commercial. That becomes ridiculous."[29]

To supplement the current data, I did some spot research of my own and looked at all the commercials shown around ITV's best-rated show, "Coronation Street" for the period 15th September 2025 – 19th September 2025.

I watched them in Blackpool, so these are the commercials that, one assumes, the media companies chose in order to target the audience who'd be tuned into the Granada TV franchise. As we'll see below, that region has a very mixed ethnicity. And one might expect the commercials to reflect that.

Anyway, here are the results: Of a total of 78 commercials which had human characters, those of South Asian appearance featured in 13, East Asian in 8 and those of black and mixed race in 43.[30] Which, however unscientific the research, might indicate...

... there's something wrong with this picture

In their defence, adlanders will tell you that the ethnic mix presented in their commercials reflects the world as they see it. After all, they live in one of the most international and ethnically mixed cities in the world.

Taking London, black people make up 13.5% and mixed race 5.7% of the capital's population. However, people of Asian origins constitute 20.8%.[31] So we find that, in over-representing people of black and mixed race heritage, the ads aren't even holding an accurate mirror to the faces we see every day on the streets of our multicultural capital.

As for places beyond the metropolis, let's look at my home town, Blackpool. In the last census black people made up just 0.5% of the population.[32] But, believe me, this doesn't make Blackpool some middle class haven of white privilege. Privilege is most commonly determined by money, power and heredity. And the main things being passed from one short-lived generation to the next in Blackpool are hopelessness and ill health. At 53.5 years, the town has the lowest male "Healthy Life Expectancy" in England.[33]

Just 17 miles away, in Preston's Deepdale Ward, 42.7% of the population identify as Indian.[34] Then again, drive 30 minutes north west and you'll be in Hambleton which, at 97.9%, is one of the whitest local authorities in England.[35]

As to Scotland, while there are long established Asian communities in Glasgow, only a few miles north east in Angus are people who haven't seen someone of mixed race since Tiger Woods last played round Carnoustie.[36]

Ethnic pockets

These are not selective snapshots. As the *New Statesman's* data journalist Ben Walker says, "Diversity in Britain is more complicated than it seems." And that's because "Britain's ethnic minorities are concentrated in England, almost entirely in a select few towns and cities, such as London, Birmingham, Luton and the urban conurbations straddling West Yorkshire and Greater Manchester."

He added: "Ethnic minorities make up more than 30% of the population in Bradford and Blackburn, for example, but more than half of neighbourhoods in both places remain more than 85 per cent white".[37]

Staying with Blackburn, the ethnic presence is actually 37.7% with 35.7% being of Asian origin and just 0.9% black. This vast discrepancy again suggests that the picture of Britain presented in our advertising is wildly distorted.[38]

If white and brown people are aware of this and are unhappy then it's too simplistic to explain away their unease as bigotry or racism.

Monetising the black presence

Their objections proceed from an awareness that they are being manipulated - in more ways than one.

Firstly, they can recognise a mercenary attempt to monetise the black presence on their screens.

This was the finding of research conducted by Koen Pauwels, distinguished professor of marketing, and Yakov Bart, associate professor of marketing, at Northeastern University.[39]

Writing in the University's global newspaper, Alëna Kuzub explained: "Bart and Pauwels hypothesize that the desire of brands to include more black actors into their ads had potentially backfired. Consumers watching the ads more carefully regarded them as not authentic and genuine but rather motivated by the perceived change in sociopolitical agenda and context.

"Under such increased scrutiny of the TV ads, the impact of racial diversity on consumer purchase intention is less likely to be positive, because consumers are more likely to perceive the brand advertisement as an inauthentic, performative or disingenuous attempt to capitalize on public attention to racial inequality."[40]

They know it's a gimmick, a fashionable posture aimed ultimately at getting them to buy more of Brand X. And they dismiss the ads accordingly.

But the danger is that others recognise something more sinister in the over-representation of black people in our advertising.

Educating the masses

We saw earlier that many of adland's leaders feel compelled to use their influence to change culture upstream in order to bring about the desired political change. They are, of course, not operating in a vacuum. And across the political/cultural spectrum, the activists' objective is to get everyone to share the progressive gaze.

Contrary to their suspicions, the masses aren't stupid. And I'd suggest there are many amongst the culturally conservative - and predominantly white - mainstream who regard the advertising and programme content as part of a broader campaign to force a progressive vision of society upon them.

Moreover, they see the casting of the commercials as but one more sign that that vision does not include them.

They feel they are being ignored by an elite who prioritise the interests of favoured minorities. And this favouritism means that, in negotiating the snakes and ladders of life in multicultural Britain, the white mainstream are left to slither downwards while those favoured minorities get a helpful leg up.

Amongst myriad other not-so-microaggressions, *their* gaze sees a judiciary operating a two tier approach to sentencing which favours minority defendants over their white counterparts[41] ... a teaching establishment where the term "Anglo-Saxon" is banned and lessons are aimed at "disrupting the centrality of whiteness"[42] ... West End theatres holding exclusively Black Out Nights "free from the white gaze"[43] ... council staff made to calculate their degree of white privilege[42] ... William Shakespeare, denounced as an agent of "white supremacy"[43] ... a BBC so committed to diversity that just one in three admitted to its flagship journalism course are white British[44] ... thousands of white, teenage girls systematically raped by predominantly Asian men, and the police and authorities doing nothing[45] ... the English countryside declared "a racist, colonial white space"[46] ... town councils removing statues of white benefactors, and museums mothballing artefacts because they speak of the sins committed by white people 250 years ago[47] ... and courts putting the interests of illegal migrants over the fears and concerns of local parents.[48]

Fueling grievances

The dice seem loaded and the game fixed. And no one senses this more acutely than the UK's biggest losers, the predominantly white working class.

You don't have to condone or endorse their resentment to accept that it is real.

As trade unionist Paul Embery writes in *Despised. Why the Modern Left Loathes the Working Class:* "There has developed a feeling within many white working class communities, not without justification, that their own traditions and culture are somehow illegitimate and must be suppressed, while they are simultaneously expected to embrace cultural diversity more generally and celebrate the particular traditions of others. Eric Kaufmann – professor of politics at University of Buckingham – has described this as 'asymmetrical multiculturalism.'"[49]

He has a point. For example, they watch as their children are handed rainbow flags to celebrate Pride Month. Then read that a 12 year old girl has been banned from attending her school's "Culture Day" for wearing a Union Jack dress.[50]

Not surprisingly, when they saw Keir Starmer and Angela Rayner taking the knee in support of Black Lives Matter, many in the working class wondered who was going to stand up for them.

Indeed, they feel abandoned by the party that was once their voice and now vilifies them for not sharing its progressive values. It's not just the politicians who've betrayed them. Keir Starmer's former director of strategy, Deborah Mattinson explained they feel "such a powerful collective sense of grievance" at the way they are treated by the metropolitan elites.[51]

Does adland care?

Much of that anger comes from the diet they are fed by those who control our broadcast media. And when they've been rendered invisible or risible by the programmes they watch and the commercials that interrupt them, is it too surprising that they question why a small minority has so much attention expended upon it?

Does adland care that a sector of society, with an already combustible feeling of isolation might feel even more alienated - and angered - by the vision it presents of everyday British life?

Likewise the Asian community's dissatisfaction with the way they are depicted on our screens. At best it's as if someone googled "South Asian culture", cut and pasted the result and stuck a logo on it. As to the East Asian presence: blink and you've missed it. In both cases, is adland concerned that we're giving the impression that black lives matter a lot more than brown ones?

And finally are we bothered that, in our rush to get as many black faces on our telly as possible, we have reduced the UK's multicultural black population to stereotypes, superfluities or simply substitutes for the white actors who used to play those parts?

I doubt it. But what is clear is that in our need to atone for our sins and impose our own skewed view of diversity, we have blundered into a minefield of race relations. And, in so doing, may well have made them more explosive.

10
Diversity and inclusion or division and intrusion?

Those on the progressive Left will tell you that the white population - and to a lesser extent, those of Asian descent - had it coming. And that equity is not just about levelling the playing field but tilting it in the favour of those designated as the oppressed.

But, as we've seen, while they purport to promote diversity and inclusion, their ideology happily excludes the most oppressed, namely the white working class.

In March 2025, the Labour peer Lord Glasman spoke for them when he said his own party's "culture has been a hostile environment for working class people. If you say what you think, then you get condemned. The inability to let people express their grief. We see people in pain and we call them far Right or populist or racist or sexist – they are just speaking."[1]

Anyone "just speaking" out against being called a "racist" would likely be accused of "white fragility" by those who see it as the defensive response of racists who are unable to confront the truth about their own prejudice.[2]

However, white fragility is a classic Kafka Trap. Derived from the eponymous author's book *The Trial*, the Kafka Trap is a logical fallacy that occurs when someone is accused of something and their protestations of innocence are used as evidence of guilt. In this case, denying the accusation that you are a racist is a sure sign that you are one.

This bit of pop psychology, conjured up by Robin DiAngelo, has little theoretical weight outside of the blind faith of those who believe in her brand of identity politics - and in the self-help book she wrote to promote her diversity consultancy.

Black fragility

Those people might do better to focus on black fragility. And how it is reinforced by identitarian politics.

Black sensitivity is, of course, understandable given the long history of oppression and the more recent discrimination they have suffered. But, in the 20th century, other of our ethnic minorities suffered worse at the hands of the British.

Take, for example, the wartime government's contribution to the 1943 Bengal Famine which killed upwards of 3 million people. Or consider the bungled dismantling of the "Raj" in 1947 which saw another million being killed in the ensuing communal violence.

Within painful living memory, people from the subcontinent experienced callous and inhumane treatment on a massive scale. Yet it doesn't seem to dominate the collective memory or individual personality of those who now live in the UK. And that's perhaps because they are not being relentlessly told that their colour is their defining attribute and that it condemns them to inescapable discrimination and second-class citizenship.

Conversely, progressive theorists have impressed this "reality" upon their black counterparts. They've been assigned the identity of "victim" and those who refuse to accept this stereotype are accused of complacency or, more viciously, of being a collaborator with the enemy and traitor to their race.

If there are penalties for not conforming to "the victim" stereotype, there are benefits for embracing it. As Ash Sarkar explains in her book *Minority Rule* "to be seen to be a victim, to be able to claim a marginalised identity position, gives you social capital ... a perch from which to speak with authority." But it can have damaging long-term effects because "we end up being attached to the social status that being a victim brings."[3]

When one's colour has been politicised in this way, is it any wonder black people are highly alert to the way it is portrayed by the media?

This sensitivity was highlighted in the ASA's Research into Ethnic Stereotyping in Advertising cited earlier. The report looked at the emphasis respondents placed on ethnicity as part of their identity, alongside other factors like age, gender, sexual orientation, marital status and religion.

And, compared to those who are Asian, mixed race and white, the black people polled were by far the most likely to see ethnicity as their most salient characteristic.[4]

Such self-consciousness means they can at times call out racism where a more objective judgement might say none exists. But when you see everything through the prism of identity politics and your oppressed status, the objective voice is often shouted down. Especially when there are progressive allies ever-ready to pile-on and do the shouting for you.

The power of the progressive pile-on

The biggest furore recently was provoked by an ad for Heinz pasta sauce. Upon its appearance - and very swift disappearance - the trade press and advertising folks on social media spoke of little else. And pretty much every word was a condemnation.

It started when VML Spain produced a poster displayed in London Underground stations which showed a wedding scene featuring the black bride sitting next to a white man who is presumably the groom.

On her right are an older white man and woman, who appear to be the groom's parents, and on her left is an older black woman who, one infers, is her mother.

Its appearance led to an outcry from critics saying the image reinforced the negative stereotype of single parent black families and the absent black dad.

One X user responded: "Total erasure of black fathers by such a mainstream brand is shocking. How did this get approved?"[5]

Alexandra Ncube, co-founder and chief executive of brand strategy firm Atom Futures, said in a LinkedIn post that the campaign had "brought outrage to many", writing: "While many may be oblivious to the blatant and subliminal harm caused by such an image, this serves as an important reminder for marketers and brand strategists to be aware of nuance and the perpetuation of negative stereotypes."[6]

The response from Heinz was instant contrition and the pulling of the ad. The advertising community went into an exaggerated bout of recrimination, the general sense being that Heinz had made a monumental tin-eared error.

A chance to "change culture" - and society

No one in adland raised the point that, intentionally or not, the poster had opened an opportunity to discuss a major societal issue.

Which is odd because for years our progressive leaders had been promoting advertising's power to "change culture". And here was an opportunity to begin a conversation which had truly transformative potential.

Because, while the pasta ad might have re-heated a stereotype, it also reflected an unfortunate truth. And a problem that blights the lives of the black community and constitutes one of UK society's biggest problems.

One of the ads main detractors Nels Abbey, the British Nigerian writer and broadcaster actually pointed this out when he wrote: "Admittedly, the stats on single parenthood look notably vicious for black communities. The figure in England and Wales increased from 48.5% in 2011 to 51.0% in 2021."

But to avoid any exploration of the cause and implications of those startling statistics, he said that fact is "a liar's best friend, and statistics on single parenthood in black communities are a bigot's closest ally." Thus ring-fencing the subject and closing down any further discussion.[7]

A colourblind problem

What a breakthrough it would have been if someone at Heinz - or any of adland's champions of social change - had responded by pointing out that the family breakdown Abbey himself alluded to is dramatically different not only across ethnic groups in the UK but also classes.

For instance, according to The Commission on Race and Ethnic Disparities, the percentage of black Caribbean children aged 0-15 living in one parent families stood at 63%. For children of the same age group in black African families, the figure was 43%.[8]

The overall figures for white English and Indian were 19% and 6% respectively. But, as we're about to see, that changes dramatically when you take class into consideration.[9]

The most deprived sector of UK society is the white working class. They have the worst educational performance record of any ethnicity. A situation which education secretary Bridget Phillipson recently described as a "national disgrace."[10]

Miriam Cates, former South Yorkshire Conservative MP says "the disparity among whites is huge. And it is explained not by skin colour but by family structure."[11] What she meant was, the vast majority of white British children in the bottom socio-economic quintile are being brought up in single parent households, with only 12% of their parents married and 9% co-habiting.[12]

The curse of dad-lessness

Whatever the causes, whatever the colour, this absent father syndrome has deep-seated ramifications for a child's life chances - and social stability.

It's not merely that these kids are more likely to drop out of school and less likely to attend university, they also are more susceptible to lifelong mental disability.[13]

The Centre for Social Justice defines family breakdown in terms of dissolution, dysfunction and 'dad-lessness'. And has warned that young people whose families break-up before they reach the age of 18 are nearly twice as likely to suffer from mental ill-health.[14]

Then, of course, there's the knife crime that is destroying so many lives in the black community. Most of it is gang-related and involves young boys who find surrogate father figures and a sense of belonging amongst their machete-wielding peers.

Clearly, then, dad-lessness in the black community and amongst the white working class has very serious outcomes. And adland having, intentionally or not, raised the subject, had the chance to open it up for debate.

Apologists for Heinz might counter by saying it was beyond the remit of a brand to initiate such a discussion. But, as I said above, for 10 years, the re-engineering of society through cultural change was the objective of the social purpose movement.

Dozens of brands have wanted to "start a conversation" about racism, the plight of refugees, loneliness among the aged, body positivism, suicide, toxic masculinity, LGBTQ+ acceptance, women's rights and, of course, the imminent environmental/biodiversity apocalypse.

As it was, having found themselves in the midst of a conversation, the people at Heinz - and their agency - fell silent, rolled over supinely and cancelled their advertising because of the progressive pile-on.

The Farage furore

This surrender to online mob rule is nothing new.

Adland's classic case came when, in July 2019, *Campaign* ran a special feature on this century's most influential UK politician, the brand building, market disruptor, Nigel Farage.[15]

Much of his popularity comes from his positioning as the tribune of the people. The un-politician who knows how to speak directly to and for the masses. You'd think that an industry that makes its living creating mass appeal for its clients might have been interested in how and why he'd been so successful.

The article tried to cast light on that with comments from such canny observers as PR guru, Mark Borkowski, Sam Delaney, author of *Mad Men and Bad Men: What Happened When British Politics Met Advertising*, Helen Thompson, professor of political economy at Cambridge University and Benedict Pringle, founder of Political Advertising UK.

There was praise for Farage's chutzpah and ambition, and how they were qualities lacking in contemporary adland. As Delaney pointed out: "From my experience of working with brands today, most campaigns start out as an exercise in damage limitation. The first goal is not to offend. And if something does offend even a handful of people, brands lose their nerve and give in."[16]

Little did he know but he was predicting exactly what happened once the article went live.

Lambasting the shit-stirrer

The usually reasonable founder of Lucky Generals, Andy Nairn, spoke for many when he said: "I don't need to see a shit-stirring, dog-whistling, race-baiting agitator who is already overexposed in the mainstream British media, smirking from the front page of my trade magazine."[17]

This was mild criticism compared to other vicious complaints. Editor-in-chief, Claire Beale, was forced to meet the progressive gaze - and blinked. Within two days she'd issued a humbling apology.[18] Indeed, I'd hazard it was this brutal experience that persuaded her to quit her role several months later.

Incidentally, according to the 17-20th October poll by More in Common, 31% of voters say they support Farage's party, Reform UK, while just 22% and 19% opt for Labour and Conservative. According to MiC, the "shit-stirrer" is set to win 373 seats and an overall majority at the next general election.[19]

Of course, his mass appeal is down to one key issue and, if the government gets its act together on immigration, they can steal his thunder. But then he'll simply shift his attention to that other highly unpopular plank in the progressive platform, net zero.

Either way he's now 9/4 with William Hill to be the next prime minister which does indicate that a lot of people think there's a lot of shit that needs stirring.[20] And that it might be wise for adland to hold its nose and find out what else is exercising the mind of this large and lucrative sector of the UK public?

I doubt that'll happen though, don't you?

Repressive Tolerance

The intolerance described above is a characteristic of the Left. In 1965, one of its iconic figures, the philosopher Herbert Marcuse, announced that in order to create a non-repressive civilization, society would need to ban alternative viewpoints that he deemed "non-tolerant." This framework was known as "Repressive Tolerance" and it has since become the core of modern progressive ideology.[21]

In the UK advertising arena, its most dedicated practitioners are the activist organisation, Stop Funding Hate (SFH).

SFH, with much of adland's tacit support, has successfully called upon dozens of companies including Marks & Spencer, John Lewis, Iceland and

Specsavers to stop advertising in newspapers whose editorial line is populist or Right of centre. Or, as its activists believe, use "fear and division to sell more papers"[22]

The prime targets have been the *Daily Express*, *Daily Mail* and *The Sun;* namely those publications that are read by the lower orders, from whom adland has been so detached for well over a decade.

Stop funding *The Spectator*

SFH claims some success in moderating the tabloid papers' coverage of the migrant crisis.[23] They had less in the row they instigated between the Co-op and *The Spectator* magazine.

From his experience of the dispute, editor Fraser Nelson explained: "The theory behind Stop Funding Hate is that publications get most of their money from advertisers, not readers - so pressure exerted via advertisers can work. If you get trolls to pose as customers, you can say 'I was a happy customer, but dismayed to see you advertise with the hateful *Daily Bugle* with all of its hate - I won't buy anymore! Boycott!'. And then, with any luck, you get the corporations to panic. If you threaten the revenue, the managers will clip journalists' wings."[24]

It didn't work with *The Spectator* because that publication gets most of its revenue from sales, not advertising. Also, the pugnacious chairman, Andrew

Neil responded to the Co-op's advertising boycott by banning the Co-op from ever advertising in the magazine again.

When the row went viral, *The Spectator* took on more new subscribers than in any single day in the magazine's 193 year history. They also got a call from the Co-op's CEO who said he knew nothing about the boycott. It seems the tweet that announced it was made by someone way down the pecking order who panicked when threatened with losing advertising revenue. Either that or they had their own political motives for cancelling *The Spectator*

The ban was swiftly lifted while the Co-op explained: "The tweet sent yesterday was incorrect and does not reflect our advertising position. Our policy supports editorial freedom and you can read more about it here."[25]

Manufacturing outrage

This raises the question of just how real was the outrage? And just how much of it was, and is, manufactured by groups of professional activists who know they can rely on a cadre of sympathisers to get angry on demand.

The boycott at *The Spectator* wasn't a grass roots thing. The Co-op's tribally Left-wing board, workforce and clientele didn't rise up in protest about ads being placed in the Right-leaning magazine.

If there were numbers objecting, Fraser Nelson speaks of "trolls" masquerading as irate members of the public.

In this case, SFH's bluff was called. But a lot of brands do succumb. And it usually isn't an ethical choice but a monetary one.

As the editor of *Spiked*, Tom Slater observed, "Regrettably, woke capital is a soft target for this kind of stuff. Businesses that don't give a stuff about politics but pretend to do so for retweets, and firms that seem to confuse Twitter argy-bargy for the public mood, are cowards and are all-too-willing to give in to those who shout the loudest online."[26]

Those doing the shouting can be relied upon to come out in numbers - either physically or virtually - once the call-to-arms has been sounded. It doesn't seem to matter who or what the object of their ire might be, just as long as it is part of the progressive omnicause. In this case, it was *The Spectator* and its views on transgender rights. It might be freedom for Palestine tomorrow and protection for asylum seekers the day after next.

The permanently angry progressive Left will fall into line whatever the issue. And as we're about to see, that applies not just to the marchers and tweeters but also to adland's movers and shakers.

"We're not talking open minds here"

Long before the channel went on air, SFH dubbed GB News the UK equivalent of Fox News, and started organising the advertising boycott.

Without seeing a single broadcast, companies like Ikea, Nivea, Kopparberg, Grolsch, Octopus Energy and the Open University complied.

Andrew Neil, who was then heading up the channel, commented "SFH started rounding up the lynch mob four months before we had even started broadcasting. So I don't think we're talking open minds here."[27]

With the ad ban hurting the station, it decided it needed to attract more viewers by doing some advertising of its own. And so, at the end of September 2021, I got a call from Wavemaker, the company that was handling GB News's media buying, asking me to write it.

I said "OK" because I liked Andrew Neil, especially after he'd put Boris Johnson to flight during the previous election campaign. The brief also appealed to my Voltairian tendency. Plus I've mates in my home town, Blackpool, who can't watch the BBC's news without having a half-brick handy.

Anyway, I wrote a poster campaign and added some press ads for an imminent nationwide launch which Wavemaker seemed to "love" and regard as "brilliant". Indeed, I was told: "We're so very excited to work with you to put GBN on the map and on the streets!"[28]

Firing your client

Then, for two weeks, silence.

Not an email, call or text.

Finally my contact at the agency phoned to tell me that not only would the much loved ads not be running but that GB News was no longer a client of the agency.

Firing a client is extremely unusual. You can be in advertising all your life and never work in an agency that makes that call.

But, as a subsequent article in *Campaign* suggested "employees and clients were resistant to the agency working for GB News and the parent company was involved in the decision to drop the client due to concerns about displeasing its other customers."[29]

Maybe the people I dealt with at Wavemaker were being admirably professional and not letting their views stop them doing their jobs properly. But I sensed they had few qualms about working with GB News. Indeed, they all seemed very excited about the ads that were about to run.

I didn't encounter Wavemaker UK's Managing Partner, James Wilde, but he had already taken to *Campaign* to say: "The primary driver behind agencies and brands boycotting the channel is that they simply don't like what it broadcasts and the audience it represents". [30]

He went on to urge his fellow planners to resist that boycott and try to empathise with the Brexit-voting provincials who were tuning into the new channel.

"It was decided at the very senior level"

The CEO of GB News, Angelos Frangopoulos, was "furious" at being fired by Wavemaker. At the pitch stage he'd insisted that any agency presenting to his board must be fully committed to the project. Wavemaker had assured him that they were.[31]

No agency embarks on a protracted pitch before working out whether it will cause conflict with other of its clients; or problems for the people who'll be servicing the business.

So it's highly unlikely the decision to terminate came from the people at Wavemaker.

As Frangopoulos told me "it was decided at the very senior level - the people we worked with were honorable and clearly embarrassed."[32]

If it was WPP's top brass who blackballed GB News then they were not only overruling the agency that had been running the account, they were ignoring the adjudicating role of the official regulatory body, Ofcom.

It is Ofcom that determines whether a broadcaster is in breach of Section 5 of its Broadcasting Code: "Due Impartiality and Due Accuracy."[33] And at the time of WPP's decision, GB News had a clean record on both counts.

That didn't bother SFH, whose advertising ban was aimed at starving GB News of the revenue needed to survive. But it should have figured in WPP's thinking. Instead, GB News was dropped and the channel was denied the expertise needed to compete fairly in the open market.

As Frangopoulos observed, "The political activism here was coming from the agency and not the broadcaster. It had allowed its own bias to sabotage a fully regulated, fully legal British media company serving a British audience".[34]

Tuning into the echo chamber

In short, WPP seems to have tuned into the echo chamber and tuned out those with differing views and values.

Which raises the question: is that wise when adland is struggling to connect with those who do not share its blinkered consensus? Indeed, isn't it self-harming for an industry that talks a lot about "being a part of culture" to cut itself off from that which it understands the least?

As Wavemaker's James Wilde had warned: "It's too easy to plan within your own media echo chamber - how will you reach those with differing political views or opinions to yourself if you do?"[35]

How indeed? And how misguided it might be to ignore an advertiser that, in August 2025, laid claim to beating BBC News and Sky News to become the most popular news channel in the UK. Moreover, beyond TV, one that has a website and app attracting an ever-growing 10.1 million people, and a radio station reaching a burgeoning 547,000 weekly listeners.[36]

Meanwhile, the boycott continues, as does adland's reluctance to challenge or criticise it.

But that's because adland's commitment to diversity is inclusive only of those issues, arguments and people with whom it agrees. Anyone or anything that doesn't conform to the progressive groupthink risks being stifled and silenced.

Or, in the famous case of Chas Bayfield and Dave Jenner, sacked.

A cautionary tale

Bayfield and Jenner were creative directors at J. Walter Thompson. Both were well respected in the industry. Bayfield especially, having been responsible for one of the greatest ads ever: the Blackcurrent Tango "St George" commercial. It won pretty much every award it was entered for in 1997 and, in May this year, was voted fifth best ad of all time by *Campaign's* A-List jury.[37]

According to court papers, at the time of their dismissals Bayfield was aged 52 and Jenner aged 50. Both were heterosexual, white and British.[38]

In a normal world, such facts shouldn't matter. But in an industry in thrall to identity politics, they bracketed those two creatives amongst Critical Theory's oppressors - and ultimately ruined their careers.

On 16 May, 2018 one of Bayfield and Jenner's creative director peers, Jo Wallace, accompanied their boss, Lucas Peon, to a conference organised by the DE+I consultancy, Creative Equals.

Wallace was there to deliver a speech that she'd written with Peon, the subject being how the agency was going to narrow the agency's yawning gender pay gap.

Much of the presentation was uncontroversial, if also hard hitting with reference to J. Walter Thompson having "a reputation as a Knightsbridge boys' club." There was also a commitment to "actively recruiting fresh female talent." So far so reasonable. Then Jo Wallace pressed the clicker and up popped this slide:

WHITE, BRITISH, PRIVILEGED, STRAIGHT MEN

CREATING TRADITIONAL ABOVE THE LINE
ADVERTISING

And to accompany this Wallace announced, "One thing we all agree on is that the reputation JWT once earnt: as being full of white, British, privileged … etc… has to be obliterated". At which the words on screen were duly, yes, obliterated.[39]

Equity in action

Note, here the thing holding the agency back was not a lack of talent, vision or creativity nor was there any hint of past failings by management. The problem was "white, British, privileged, straight men". And the solution? Well, as Critical Theorists intended, the workplace was to be divided in terms of identity, with retributive justice (obliteration) to be exacted in the name of equity.

When news of this hit the creative department, Jenner and Bayfield contacted Peon, Kate Bruges the UK and Europe learning & development director and HR director, Emma Hoyle to voice unease about the language used in the speech.

At a subsequent meeting Hoyle tried to explain that it was the reputation that was to be obliterated, not the members of staff. Whereby the two creatives argued that you couldn't obliterate the reputation without dismissing people on grounds of their identity. Suffice to say, both sides later described the encounter as "angry" and even "horrible".[40]

Within two days Bayfield and Jenner's names had been added to a list of those being lined up for a round of cost-saving redundancies.

Crucially, when Lucas Peon saw that list, he asked for the name of one female colleague to be removed. According to court records, he accepted that this was because "he wanted to save her from redundancy because she was a woman; he agreed that 'he took sex into account'".[41]

In other words, it was her favoured status amongst the oppressed identities and not her talent that kept her on the payroll.

There was no such reprieve for Jenner and Bayfield. On June 11th they received the letter beginning the process that led to their redundancy and the court case which saw them winning claims of sex discrimination, victimisation, harassment and unfair dismissal.

Alternative points of view "angrily dismissed"

It's noteworthy that in summing up, judge Mark Emery highlighted the intolerance of those who were running what had, by then, become Wunderman Thompson. And he seemed shocked by the aggressive response to Bayfield and Jenner's argument.[42]

The judge said: "Both Ms Hoyle and Mr Peon were angry from the outset of the meeting, and it continued in this vein. Voices were raised by Mr Peon and Ms Hoyle, and Mr Bayfield and Mr Jenner were forced to defend their position. Their explanations were not at the time accepted and their points of view were angrily dismissed."[43]

Bayfield and Jenner were treated this way because they had questioned the groupthink. And we know that the progressive Left brooks little resistance on that front - especially if those doing the resisting are deemed to be part of the oppressor identity.

As Bayfield said, "The gender pay gap was mortifying for the company - because it was an awful gap - and their approach was to go gung-ho on who they perceived to be the enemy. They rigged up a kangaroo court and fired us."[44]

"I remember feeling like I just had a target on my back. I remember thinking, if I was a black 24-year-old woman I'd be fine. If I had been gay, even better."[45]

The corruption of the diversity economy

Jenner's lawyer, QC Adrian Scotland, said at the time: "The experiences outlined in this case are sadly commonplace. It is a growing part of the work we do day-to-day.

"Every good thing is vulnerable to corruption and with the billions poured into the diversity economy it should be no surprise that there are more and more bad actors appearing."

The lawyer also added, "Hopefully the judgment will encourage more people to stand up to the 'Cancel Club' and rediscover their value as individuals in promoting a tolerant and all-inclusive society."[46]

Jenner and Bayfield's subsequent experience made that highly unlikely.

Jenner struggled to find a permanent position and, for a while, quit the industry.

In a 2021 interview, Bayfield said he himself had "not worked a huge amount" in the last three years and had "certainly never achieved the level he was at with JWT".

He'd also decided to emigrate "partly due to being made redundant", the decision being "massively accelerated by the absence of work over here."

In his view, both he and Jenner had suffered because they were considered as "whistleblowers by the industry".[47]

Others who might blow the whistle on dodgy DE+I dealings will have noted their fate.

As QC Adrian Scotland said at the time of the hearing, they had "risked their careers to take on a global corporation with the reach and influence of WPP."[48] And, as a result, it's highly unlikely they'll ever again find permanent jobs at senior level with any of the dozens of agencies owned by that holding company. Or any other.

He's Spartacus

Anyone brave or foolhardy enough to emulate Bayfield and Jenner nowadays would join them in advertising purgatory.

Never working again is the long-term deterrent. But there's also an immediate emotional and financial cost.

I know this first hand because I was once involved in litigation with one of the big holding companies. And my direct adversary was the CEO who'd assumed personal responsibility for the case.

Going up against a determined opponent with seemingly limitless resources is pretty frightening - especially when simply receiving an email from your own brief can cost you £500 or more.

Thankfully the case was settled swiftly and amicably. But mine did not have the potential for damning reputational damage that would surround a case related to DE+I. And, given today's politicisation of the workplace, no agency or network would allow itself to lose one of those cases without digging deep into its coffers - and potentially bankrupting the other party.

There are probably scores of individuals who'd like their day in court. Over the past 10 years, people of the same unfavoured identity as Bayfield and Jenner have got used to the casual abuse that's directed at them. One exec remembers "waiting for a senior leadership team meeting at one of the larger UK agencies to start. The global CEO bowled into the meeting room, late, looked mildly disgusted and said 'isn't this a disappointing gathering of middle-aged, white men' (This was when the business was growing by 20% year-on-year, had record profits, was doing well on the awards front and had a happy and well-remunerated workforce.) But what we got was the triple whammy of ageism, racism and sexism in one sentence!"[49]

That was mild in comparison to the career-threatening prejudice faced by many "middle-aged white men". But they've remained silent because the professional, financial and emotional costs involved in bringing such cases to court would be too high. Moreover, if any of them did so, they know they'd be enjoying a lonely martyrdom. Because in today's workplace, the collective response would be a prudent "He's Spartacus!"

Can you see this ad being made today?

In one way, Chas Bayfield was lucky. At least "St George", the commercial that brought him fame and lots of awards, got made.[50]

It's doubtful it would survive the first work in progress meeting today.

Let's begin with the title, "St George" and, oh dear, we're on dodgy ground already.

Someone in the agency (not necessarily involved in the ad) would say it's inflammatory. And point out that many people nowadays are threatened by the cross of St George and find it divisive and intimidating. Indeed, as I write, Left-wing dominated councils from Birmingham to Brighton are pulling down those being flown by members of the public.[51]

Then, gulp, there's the script

It starts with the Tango rep from customer service talking to camera about a letter he has received from a French student criticising the new Blackcurrant Tango.

As his response becomes ever more passionate, he marches out of the office and across the car park where he starts stripping off his clothes to reveal a pair of purple boxing shorts.

Bare chested, he climbs into a boxing ring on the very edge of the emblematic, White Cliffs of Dover and challenges the French student, the French nation and, indeed, the whole of Europe to a fight. As an assembled crowd of flag-waving supporters cheer wildly, three Harrier jump jets with purple landing lights hover into view.

Even back in 1996 *Campaign* thought the ad was "controversial". And, writing in *The Independent*, cultural commentator Peter York explained why: "Tango has joined the Referendum Party and is sworn to kick out Johnny Frenchman. The launch of Blackcurrant Tango provides the opportunity for a fizzy drink to make a unique political statement - indeed an intervention. The European Movement will no doubt object strenuously."[52]

For the above mentioned "Referendum Party" read today's Reform UK. And try to imagine an agency producing an ad that might even tangentially be linked to Nigel Farage's politics. Or, one that gave vent to, in York's words, "chauvinist hysteria".

Then ask yourself who, in today's pearl-clutching adland, would toy with, even jokingly, expressing any kind of exaggerated patriotism? If they did, they'd censor themselves before the idea ever made it to script form. And, in the unlikely event of the idea ever materialising, the Tango spokesperson would have morphed into a mixed race member of the LGBTQ+ community and the script would be paean to European unity.

It would also be lacking any vestige of what made the original so popular.

Fun.

Is irreverence too dangerous?

In the hyperserious, politicised workplace, fun is in short supply. This feeds into the work and has damaged the industry.

I remember Dave Trott advising us on LinkedIn: "If you understand ordinary people, you would then understand they don't care about advertising. So the real question is, how to get ordinary people to care about what we do? And the answer is entertainment. The answer is to make it fun … Maybe if we could remember how trivial advertising is, we could remember it's our job to make it interesting and fun".[53]

In the same week, Sir John Hegarty explained that the best business advice he'd had "came from a greengrocer who said, 'When they're not smiling, they're not buying.' I think he's right. We should never overlook the power of humour. Especially its potential to connect."[54]

I was at an award ceremony where Sir John provided the entertainment with an onstage interview. At the end, he was asked what single quality made for truly successful, memorable advertising.

Sir John thought for a few seconds and said: "Irreverence".

We then went upstairs to see pretty much all the awards going to social purpose campaigns that had not a scintilla of irreverence amongst them. I recall racing to the bar as the last gong was handed out muttering "kill me now".

I was also left wondering, is irreverence too risky nowadays? After all, one person's irreverence is another's microaggression. Or, in the case of the latest poster campaign for American Eagle: "Eugenics. Nazi propaganda. And its [sic] BLATANT."[55]

This Instagram post was prompted by the sight of actress Sydney Sweeney clad in American Eagle's denims above the headline stating she "has great jeans". It was one of many, as self-identifying Left-leaning activists and influencers hit the keys to call out the campaign's white supremacist message. Conservatives then hailed the ads as landing a blow against woke advertising.[56]

Less excitable critics pointed out that it wasn't the world's greatest advertising campaign. But the mere announcement that Sweeney would be appearing had made American Eagle's stock jump as much as 12% in New York.[57]

And sales no doubt benefited from the publicity prompted by the social media outrage.

The folks at American Eagle seemed mystified by that response. On their website they spoke about Sweeney's "ability to not take herself too seriously".[58] Or, in other words, her irreverence. American Eagle hadn't realised that that's not a quality you can use too freely without offending someone's progressive sensibilities.

Banning banter

This censorious approach has killed off the lighthearted banter that once characterised agency life. And, in turn, has blunted our creative edge.

I'd suggest it was this competitive, verbal back 'n' forth that helped hone the deft wordsmithery that made British copywriting the envy of the world.

For instance, have a look through the *D&AD Copy Book* which celebrates the work of 50 of advertising's best writers. You'll see evidence of the office culture of combative backchat in headlines like: "'I never read The Economist' - Management Trainee aged 42" … "We stole their land, their buffalo and their women.

Then we went back for their shoes" ... "The expandable suitcase. Now you can steal the bathrobe as well as the toiletries" ... "Here's my dead dog. Where's my award?" ... "Easily embarrassed? Wear a wotsit and no one will know you've got a thingy" ... "Somebody mentions Jordan. You think of a Middle Eastern country with a 3.3% growth rate" ... "It's not the winning. It's the taking apart."[59]

Most have elements of the put-down and one-upmanship that were the soul of office repartee.

I say "were" because people are now afraid to direct even a mildly mocking barb at a colleague in case it results in an employment tribunal.

And that pressure will surely increase under the Employment Rights Bill. Once this is passed into law, employees who feel they have been offended by casual office chat will be entitled to hold their employer to account.

Which means businesses will have to police office conversation in order to stay out of court.

Mind your language

The most innocuous turn of phrase is already construed as a provocative slight.

I had one young planner tell me that he was reprimanded by his line manager for asking "Who's doing the donkey work?"[60] The reasoning for the warning was vague but had something to do with denigrating the role played by a colleague and reinforcing the agency's hierarchical structures.

Fear of misspeaking can dog even the most senior people in the industry. Ogilvy Chairman Rory Sutherland has said: "You can have a brilliant reputation and have earned the respect of your industry and peers. But one sentence in a speech you made six months ago in Belgrade can be held against you and instantly destroy your career."[61]

He sees that intimidatory power being wielded by the "Commissariat". And recently described the grip it now has on the industry. "When I was hired at 22, I was chosen by people who were or later became acclaimed in the field of advertising. What I'm most worried about now is being put on notice by HR for misgendering someone's dog."[62]

Obviously, creativity suffers when such caution prevails.

One CEO told me" Everyone's very outwardly 'friendly'. But it is forced. There's a sense that no one can afford to offend anyone because of heightened sensitivities. But I really miss the creative directors communicating their passion and driving the department forward. Not bullying, of course. They weren't shouting at *the person*. It was about *the work,* and showing how much it meant to them. Sometimes it's the only way you get a team to turn a 7 out of 10 to a 9 out of 10. By pushing people onwards. And that's missing now."[63]

There are limits to how far a team can go - or be pushed. An award-winning creative duo explained, "It is impossible now to start with a blank screen and an open mind. We keep having to ask ourselves 'Can we say that?'" And, as we saw when analysing the *St George* ad for Tango, the answer would probably be, "No we can't".[64]

You can lose your job if you criticise DE+I

There are also other *verba non grata* - those that criticise this kind of DE+I departmental overreach.

I was in one London agency speaking to a board member about the state of the advertising world. When I asked him about the effectiveness of his agency's DE+I policies, this usually expansive individual instinctively looked nervously around our empty room and lowered his voice.

No wonder he was apprehensive. There is a general feeling in the industry that to publicly question the prevailing dogma is to jeopardise one's career. You'll have noticed that I have not identified the person above or, indeed, many of the agency personnel I've quoted throughout this book. Reason is, they're scared.

Likewise, as I mentioned on page 13, no one from a major agency was willing or able to respond to my LinkedIn posts bemoaning the pernicious impact of social purpose.

That's because, nowadays, HR's background checks are verifying much more than what's on your cv and who's giving you a reference.

I've had the CEO of a major media company tell me that he'd lose his job if he was seen to leave a supportive comment on one of my posts that criticised the way DE+I was being applied in the industry.

Another person wrote to me: "With regards to HR, I am less concerned about them actively monitoring me and more worried I'll have it from someone who views my work profile here [on LinkedIn] and reaches out to them to cause trouble."[65]

That's right. The online censors are willing to contact their target's employers, the aim being to not just silence them but get them the sack.

Which gives us the absurd situation where worker is pitted against worker in the very name of diversity and inclusion. Meanwhile the employer is empowered to discipline an employee for something they do in their free time.

Call it Kafkaesque ... Orwellian ... Stalinist. Pick your trope. But adland seems to have institutionalised a groupthink and created a bureaucracy and a cadre of informers to enforce it.

I should also add, to *entrench* it. Recent events have proven that the "Commissariat" has plenty of apparatchiks who, as I said earlier, are willing to die on the hill for DE+I.

11
Doubling down on DE+I

We started this book in November 2024 with the Jaguar film and the outcry that signalled the passing of social purpose.

We've also seen how its advocates have regrouped around the cause of Diversity, Equity + Inclusion.

Yet a few days prior to the Jag launch, the ground upon which they were making their stand was shaken by a much more seismic event.

On November 5th, Donald J. Trump was elected 47th President of the United States.

Immediately after his inauguration he addressed a joint session of Congress and announced: "We have ended the tyranny of so-called diversity, equity and inclusion policies all across the entire federal government and, indeed, the private sector and our military. And our country will be woke no longer."[1]

Within days, the leading lights of woke capitalism had started dismantling DE+I.

ESG, DE+I, RIP?

On February 25th, BlackRock, the pioneer of ESG and ethical investing, dropped all reference to DE+I from its latest annual report, three years after the company's CEO Larry Fink said the company "must embed DEI into everything we do."[2]

Another of Wall Street's champions of ESG and DE+I, JP Morgan Chase's Jamie Dimon angrily announced he was never a "firm believer" in bias training. "I saw how we were spending money on some of this stupid s—, and it really pissed me off … I'm just gonna cancel them. I don't like wasted money in bureaucracy."[3]

On February 28th, State Street Global Advisors abandoned previous targets for the number of women and minority directors who should serve on corporate boards. This was the same State Street that won a record four Grands Prix and a total of 18 Lions at Cannes in 2017. The gong magnet was the "Fearless Girl" statue that State Street and its agency McCann, New York had erected in Manhattan's financial district in its campaign to increase gender diversity in business.[4]

Legal pressure, voluntary action

At the same time, such companies as Goldman Sachs, Victoria's Secret, Meta, Warner Bros, Harley-Davidson, Ford, Walmart and *The Wall Street Journal* started walking, nay, running away from such DE+I initiatives as employer mandated bias training, participation in external diversity surveys, pronoun identification and tying executive bonuses to diversity targets.[5]

Even before Trump signed his Executive Order, US companies had been under extreme legal pressure to dial down on DE+I.

The most important was the Supreme Court's June 2023 decision, Students for Fair Admissions v. Harvard, which ruled that race-based affirmative action programmes in college admissions violate the equal protection clause of the Fourteenth Amendment.

That decision and Trump's war on woke then emboldened opponents who had previously remained silent. Indeed, Meir Shemla, associate professor of organisational behaviour at Rotterdam School of Management, reckoned Trump's opposition to DE+I was set to "amplify an undercurrent of scepticism that has been building for years".[6]

Spreading to the UK

It was an undercurrent that carried UK businesses in the same direction.

Here they are under no political pressure to abandon DE+I. Indeed they are operating under a Labour Government that is wholly supportive of its proliferation.

But if Wall Street led the retreat in the US then similar manoeuvres were ongoing in London's financial district.

In late January 2025, the Institute & Faculty of Actuaries (IFoA) abandoned plans to introduce its own strict diversity rules after a revolt by some members.[7]

Then, in early March, the UK's top financial regulators, the Financial Conduct Authority and the Prudential Regulation Authority, said they would not be proceeding with plans requiring financial services companies to report more data on employees' age, ethnicity, gender, religion and sexual orientation.[8]

"There's no way regulators should be wasting their time asking for data or challenging [bankers] on it," said one City veteran. "I doubt there is a boss brave enough to speak out, but once the vibe shift kicks in, you'll find they all suddenly do."[9]

Yes, that's right, another "vibe shift"

We've seen how the last one affected social purpose. And how adland was reluctant to accept that its moment had passed.

Well, it was equally slow to recognise the mood might have turned against DE+I.

Indeed, predictably, industry leaders lined up to make sure that that particular Overton Window remained fixed firmly in its ideological architrave.

First off was Bee Pahnke, creative director and head of voice at Grey London with her *Campaign* article:

"Brands – in this era of culture wars, don't give up on DEI&R".[10]

Her main argument was that those customers who reside in the intersectional pyramid of oppression - and therefore most in need of DE+I initiatives - will reward the brands who stick with them.

Then Bee rather undermined the idea that those with protected characteristics were suffering too much in the way of oppression when she ran off these stats:

"The global spending power of LGBT+ people was recently estimated to be $3.9tn by Bloomberg. The collective economic power of black consumers is to expand to $1.7tn by 2030. Women are to own 75% of the world's discretionary spend by 2028, and the 1.3 billion disabled people globally, along with their friends and family, are worth $13tn to brands."[11]

Which indicated there must be a lot of "oppressed" people who are doing rather well. And, of course, a lot of others who are not.

Or, in other words, you could lump together the LGBT+, black, women and disabled who are doing OK and label them "middle class". And you could take those who aren't and label them "working class or underclass".

And if you did that, and you were interested in social justice, it might be more effective if you abandoned the division of society on grounds of identity and instead went back to solving the inequalities caused by class division.

Which is a thought we'll return to later.

Framing the argument, yet again

Other *Campaign* features followed, like "Diversity is not a dirty word"[12] ... "Has big business lost its mind or just its principles?"[13] ... and "How can UK adland champion DE&I in the Donald Trump era?"[14]

The latter was the big one with seven advertising luminaries lining up to offer their views.

Note from the headline that *Campaign's* editorial staff were in no doubt about adland's role as the champion DE+I. I said previously that progressives have used their influence within our institutions to frame the arguments for us - and here is a classic example.

One assumes little effort was made to find an alternate point of view. So what we got was mostly a chorus of righteous disapproval of any criticism of DE+I. Plus some of the pious platitudes that characterised the commentary referenced on pages 45 to 49.

There were a couple of veiled hints that the current approach to DE+I might need improving. The first came from Asad Dhunna, founder and chief executive of The Unmistakables (and last seen in IPA's Palace of Westminster debate on page 94) who argued for an "inclusive culture where anyone from any background can contribute and do their best work in a place that keeps them connected with the world. After all, isn't that Trump's MO when it comes to "meritocracy"?[15]

The fact that he was open to "anyone from any background" was an improvement on the reflexive fixation with the favoured identities.

And there was this from Lameya Chaudhury of Lucky Generals: "Too many outsiders don't know what we do, and the talent we need - diverse, switched-on, and culturally fluent - don't see themselves in our work or in the teams making it."[16]

The acknowledgement that "too many outsiders don't know what we do" might just have been a forward step away from the focus on the usual suspects.

But I think we're clutching at straws here in search of some kind of balance.

Putting politics before public duty

Having said that, we come away empty-handed from *The Drum's* coverage.

Some 23 industry leaders were asked to comment on Meta's decision to reform its DE+I programme. Every single one voiced opposition to such a move. Zoe Eagle, the CEO at Iris fell back on that old standard: "It's a moral imperative." Rupert Pick the co-founder of Hot Pickle warned: "In my 20 years in marketing, I've never seen society regress like this." While Laura Kay Lambert announced "This is a terrifying shift."[17]

It wasn't just the agencies behaving like this. In a classic act of repressive tolerance, TfL (Transport for

London) dumped Accenture Song/Droga 5 from the agencies pitching for their business because they'd rowed back on their own commitment to DE+I.[18]

You'd think that a publicly funded business like TfL owed it to its major stakeholder [the public] to prioritise finding a supplier who delivered the best service. But apparently Accenture's research, strategic and creative capabilities were of no consequence.

It's hard to decouple TfL's commitment to DE+I from the progressive politics of its chairman, Mayor Sadiq Khan. So it would be disingenuous to deny that the decision to ditch Accenture Song was anything but political.

Suffice to say, no one in the ad industry said that this was coercive - not just to Accenture but to every other agency involved with TfL. And no one rose to a fellow agency's defence. Or even questioned the decision. Indeed, in the trade press, it was applauded as a "reason to be cheerful".[19]

But what do you expect, when the belief system that informed TfL's decision has been endorsed and promoted by every advertising industry institution? There's simply no need or room for debate.

We're out of sync with the public

Which is a problem because the great mass of UK citizens do not share this obsession with diversity and inclusion. Yes, they might nod their heads in support when asked a straight "Yes/No" test of their level of tolerance. But salience is everything. And when placed in the context of personally important issues, frankly, they don't really care.

For example, prior to the July 2024 general election a survey featuring in "Woke vs Anti-Woke? Culture War Divisions and Politics," from King's College, London asked "Which issues will determine your vote?"

Some 43% ticked "Cost of living", 28% chose "Health and social care/NHS" and 13% chose "Asylum seekers crossing the channel".

There were 21 options to choose from. And bottom with 1% was "Transgender rights". Below that were "Race relations" and "Women's rights" which registered an unmeasurable negligible response.[20]

Can advertising do mass marketing anymore?

The significance of adland's unquestioning support for DE+I and the public's scepticism and even opposition was pointed out, with typical acuity, by Nick Asbury:

"Following Trump's inauguration speech, generally respected pollster Opinium asked British voters to react to excerpts while concealing the identity of the speaker. When it came to the DEI section that read 'We will end the government policy of trying to socially engineer ethnicity and gender into every aspect of public and private life. We will forge a society that is colour-blind and merit-based,' the majority of British voters agreed (53% in favour, 23% against.)

"Add these British people to the 77 million citizens who voted for Trump, who increased his vote share with all ethnic groups apart from whites, and you don't get a picture of overwhelming support for doubling down on DEI. But somehow that perspective is absent from the industry press ... Is there no piece, anywhere, that is even mildly DEI-sceptical in the same way that the mainstream appears to be?

"In the ad industry, I don't see any serious reckoning with the huge data point of an election involving 156 million voters – nothing but doubling down on a narrow agenda with narrow public support.

"Can adland do the job of mass-marketing if it's so wilfully disconnected from the masses?"[21]

You could ask the same question when you consider the industry's partisan position on most of the issues that coalesce round diversity and inclusion.

Take transgender rights for instance

You'll recall that in April 2025 the Supreme Court ruled that the definition of sex as used in the Equality Act of 2010 is "binary" and decided by biology. Which means that a person not born as a biological female cannot obtain the legal protections the Act affords to women by changing their gender with a Gender Recognition Certificate.[22]

BBH led adland's resistance with talk of a "trans legal crisis" and left a rainbow decorated toilet outside the Supreme Court.[23]

I had the temerity to indirectly enter the debate myself. Or should I say, attempt to start one. *The Telegraph* had asked me to write some topical headlines for their poster and digital campaign. One of which read: "Should athletes born as men be muscling in on women's sport?"

A few dozen people thought this too provocative and complained to the ASA who tacitly reminded them they live in a country where there's freedom to discuss such issues.

They might also have pointed out that the governing bodies of major sports in England - football, cricket, netball, hockey, athletics, golf, cycling, rugby, pool and swimming - were answering the question posed in the headline by imposing bans on trangender women.[24]

As is often the case, the public had been ahead of the game. Even before the High Court ruling, 74% supported the view that transgender women no longer be allowed to play in women's teams in England.

Just 12% thought it wrong, and clearly most of them went on to read a LinkedIn post that featured my headline.[25]

"This fills me with so much rage"

The post said the headline was "designed to stoke bigotry and hate". It was liked by 123 people, many of whom work in advertising and marketing.

The majority were in very violent agreement that the poster was "hate speech", "aggressively transphobic" and "an evil strategy". One correspondent was moved to say: "This fills me with so much rage."[26]

Such was the vitriolic response to a question that the vast majority of people in this country would consider totally reasonable.

But it crossed adland's red lines on diversity and inclusion, so what do you expect?

We're actually incredibly conservative

In the splenetic anger described above, you see the industry's reflexive response to every progressive call to arms.

You might recall over 80 creative and media agencies came out for eco-truant, Greta Thunberg, at the height of the 2019 Global Strike for Climate demonstrations.[27] And how, when Black Lives Matter hit the headlines, the entire industry fell in step and took the knee.[28]

On both occasions, no one from our agencies or institutions suggested that it might be possible to want to a) do something about the climate crisis and b) fight racism and still have distinct reservations about both of those hard line, militant movements.

And again the reason lies in our politics. As Ali Hanan, founder and chief executive of Creative Equals, has said, "Let's not forget we are one of the most progressive advertising communities in the world."[29]

Politically yes! Who would doubt that.

But, as I have tried to point out, the imposition of the progressive gaze means everyone sees the world in exactly the same way. And to stultifying effect.

This was the point made last May by Simon Daglish, the deputy managing director at commercial ITV: "We've become, as an industry, incredibly conservative. We massively lack diversity. And I'm not talking about the pigment of your skin or your sexuality. I'm talking about your thought process. We've become really Victorian in our views, and we all think and believe the same thing."[30]

The use of the "c" word as a descriptor would probably provoke progressives to new heights of apoplexy.

As would the suggestion that there is a way to break out of their radical rut.

And that is, quite simply, to start hiring a lot more political and cultural conservatives from amongst mainstream and, in particular, the working class.

12
The barbarians at the gate

This brings me back to the point raised on page 130. We need to focus on class not identity. And, in so doing, abandon the ideology that has informed our efforts to re-engineer the industry - and society.

There is, after all, much evidence to suggest that class has a greater effect on an individual's life chances than skin colour.

For example, the landmark 2024 report, "Shaping our Economy" is the largest survey into socio-economic diversity and career progression ever under-taken in the UK.[1]

In all, 149,111 people (or nearly one fifth of those working in the UK Financial Services) took part in the study which concluded that "Among all combinations of gender and ethnicity, those who are from higher socio-economic backgrounds are much more likely to be found in the most influential roles in UK financial services."

In other words, as we've found in advertising, the elites retain control regardless of their colour or their gender.

"The evidence is clear. Progression and hiring are heavily influenced by attributes that have little or no correlation with job performance, but which are more available to those from higher socio-economic backgrounds. This includes drawing on family and alumni networks, and on cultural preferences that have currency in a profession that has been shaped over many years by this dominant group."[2]

Class, networks and nepotism

Research, published by KPMG in December 2022, also showed socio-economic background has a greater impact on career progression than any other diversity characteristic.[3]

The following year, KPMG did a study of 2,000 adolescents and found that they also ascribe a lack of career opportunities to social class - with the added problem of nepotism favouring their more affluent and better connected peers.[4]

This seems to be the overarching view - and one held by those who've confronted both racial and class barriers to advancement.

As the authors of Policy Exchange's "A Portrait of Modern Britain Ethnicity and Religion" explain: "Ethnic minority individuals overwhelmingly thought that class was more important than race in determining whether a person would succeed in modern day Britain (54% class vs 26% race). This held true over every ethnic group polled."[5]

Adland's champions of diversity tend to agree as well.

Supercharging disadvantage

Class was seen as the biggest barrier by Kevin Darton who, for eight years, was course leader in Creative Advertising at the University of Central Lancashire in Preston.

Given the town's large immigrant population, Kevin was well aware of the difficulties that race can present to his students. But he was adamant that any disadvantage is "supercharged" by class. "Being from the working class acts as a multiplier to the other obstacles a student might encounter."[6]

That's been the experience of two young Asian creatives, Finza Aslam and Aaliyah Rice who have been trying to make the transition from college to agency.

In an interview they did with Kevin, Aaliyah explained that class was "the first difference we see when we walk through the door. I think our biggest achievement has been working out of our class mould, not necessarily breaking from our ethnic minority or being women in the industry. Finza agreed: "It's such a massive achievement, but it's also incredibly difficult to do."[7]

"We're in danger of becoming a monocultural profession"

Actually, for working class youngsters, just getting into a college is incredibly difficult.

As the 2023 All Party Parliamentary Group for Creative Diversity research found, "Youngsters from a managerial and middle class background make up over half of all applications, offers and acceptances on creative courses. Those whose families are manual labouring working class have the worst applications-to-offers-to-acceptance ratios than any other social group."[8]

In our industry we should be thankful for the Brixton Finishing School which is dedicated to giving working class kids the start they need.

When its graduates and applicants were asked about the barriers to entry into the industry, the headlines were made by the 31% who cited race as the main obstacle.

But over twice as many (71%) said "not knowing the right people" was the biggest problem. Nepotism and networking guarantee the scions of the middle class a place at London's agencies. If you're not from that class and don't have those connections, you don't have much of a chance.[9]

That was back in 2020. More recent research by VCCP and the Account Planning Group (APG) indicates that, for all the obsessive talk of diversity and inclusion, things haven't improved. And the problems are much worse for working class kids from outside London.

"Just over a third (35%) of young people from working class backgrounds outside London know somebody working in the creative sector, compared with over half (54%) of people from more advantaged backgrounds in London and the south-east."[10]

And you can bet that many of those London-based connections would be tapped-up for a placement or an internship.

Indeed, 67% of those who knew someone in the sector stated they could "see themselves forging a successful career" in the creative industries.[11]

Apparently the working class kids' view of those who did make it in the creative industries had them down as "middle class, excessively ruthless and arrogant".[12]

Which, given some of the people we've met over the preceding pages, ain't that far off the mark.

Summing up, Sarah Newman, director of the APG, said: "There are huge regional and socio-economic disparities which make brands and agencies impenetrable to excellent people disadvantaged by geography and a lack of industry know-how."

Michael Lee, chief strategy officer at the VCCP Partnership, adds: "Right now, because of the increasing socio-economic barriers to entry, we're in danger of becoming a monocultural profession."[13]

With all due respect to Michael and the work he's been doing, I think we got there some time ago.

Why the workers won't be welcome

VCCP and the APG were talking about a colour blind version of the working class which includes a huge contingent from the white section of UK society.

Unfortunately the progressive Left wrote off these dumb Brexit-choosing, Boris-backing, *Express*-reading, Reform-voting, flag-waving, migrant-fearing, Red Wall red necks long ago.

And unless there is an industry-wide vibe shift, their flat vowels and provincial views will - like criticism of adland's current DE+I orthodoxy - remain unheard in Shoreditch and Southwark's bastions of progressive privilege.

To begin with, the activists and careerists who'll die on the hill in defence of DE+I, won't want to share that moral high ground with people they deem undeserving of a helping hand up.

Lawyer and essayist Alan Flanagan explained why when he observed: "There is one crucial fact underpinning this lack of class-based conscience among progressives: the vast majority of working class voters lack the requisite concentration of melanin to qualify them for the benevolent paternalism of progressivism."[14]

To suddenly embrace the predominantly white working class would be a denial of the progressives' belief in a society neatly divided between those who do the oppressing and those that are oppressed.

As we've seen, these groups are defined by their racial, ethnic, gender and ableist identity and not socio-economic status. And thus, in the progressive gaze, identity trumps class when deciding who is deserving of help and who's deserving of hate.

If "hate" seems like too strong a word, try "despise". That is how firefighter and trade union activist Paul Embery describes the attitude of the progressive Left to the working class. When, that is, they aren't expressing a "sneering mockery". As he says, "Today's Labour Party treats them as if they are an embarrassing relative. It still wants their votes but it doesn't want to be seen in public with them. Their views are antediluvian and reactionary."[15]

Embery was writing in 2021 when, in response to this treatment, the working classes had switched their allegiance to Johnsonian Conservatism. That was bad enough, as far as progressives were concerned. But now they've found an outlet for their "antediluvian and reactionary" views in the ascendant Reform party.

And you've got to ask yourself how would an influx of such working class people be regarded in middle class adland?

Faragophobia

We've already seen how the industry treats the amplifier of those "antediluvian and reactionary" views, GB News. Few agencies are willing to question

Stop Funding Hate's attempts to bankrupt and kill off the working class's news channel of choice.

And remember WPP HQ's reaction to the news that one of its media shops was disgracing itself by associating with GB News? Rather than work with a channel that spoke to and for a primarily working class audience, the biggest advertising network in the world did everything in its power to silence it.

One of GB News's most popular voices is, yes, Nigel Farage. And we saw on page 162 how the industry feels about him! To this day the editors of *Campaign* are still too ashamed/afraid to feature *that* article in their archive.

But, according to figures that predate this summer's asylum hotels furore, some 38% of working class people intend to vote for his party, Reform while 17% say Conservative. Which means 55% of the former bedrock Labour support are now what progressives like to call "hard Right".[16]

Can you imagine the reception they'd receive if the ad industry opened its doors to large swathes of these people?

Working class chameleons

Former Labour Party press secretary Alastair Campbell described the outsiders' dilemma in his June 2025 *Guardian* article "If you went to state school, do you ever feel British life is rigged against you?"

"Some 93% of working class professionals say their background clashes with workplace culture … To fit in, people say they start to change. Accent. Clothes. Hobbies. Even what they eat and drink."[17]

They must also change the way they think - or at least continuously edit what they say. Which means that if they want to join today's white collar workforce they must adopt the metropolitan persona of, in David Goodhart's term, "someone from anywhere". And abandon their old parochial identity as "someone from somewhere."[18]

As Campbell continued: "While a lot of this happens quietly - with a smile, a nod, a stiff upper lip mentality - the impact is loud and lasting; 61% of respondents said they had to leave their community behind to progress. Nearly half said their friendships changed. Some grew distant from their families. This is not social mobility - it's a social trade-off.

"The question now is: do we want a country where success still depends on knowing the right people, sounding the right way and fitting into the right mould? Or do we want one where talent is prized and diversity of thought guaranteed?"[19]

The crucial final point here is "diversity of thought". That comes only when you encourage people to bring their experiences, views and values with them when they go to work. And to feel as if they can express them openly without fear of ridicule or ostracism.

Campbell was talking about what's happening in the general office arena. According to James Hillhouse his observations are absolutely applicable to our industry.

Alienation in adland

James runs Commercial Break, an organisation that works with agencies to increase the number of working class people they have on their books. And, crucially, to help integrate them so they can make the most of this opportunity.

He says that many undergo the same alienating experience that Campbell described. And it goes something like this: "These people are different from me, they look different to me, they sound different to me. When they go home they go home to people the same as them. I've never met this group before, so I just don't belong here."

As a result, they either leave or, as described above, they mutate. Apparently, when one of James's protegees went home after work his Mum would tell him: "Now take that face off."

As James concludes: "You've got to go in and pretend to be someone else." And, in the process, become strangers to the people you've left behind. And embarrassed by them."[20]

Ashamed of being working class

This, in itself, reflects a huge societal change. Because, to James's parents "being working class was a badge of honour and I grew up to believe that being working class was a superpower. But now too many people in our industry are ashamed and can't talk about it."[21]

A key reason, I'd suggest, is that until the 1990s we had a Labour movement that represented the working class, promoted its interests and celebrated its virtues.

As we've seen, today, the progressive Left has disparaged and disowned it.

The upshot being, any newcomer to London agency life would be wise to adopt the opinions that inform adland's groupthink. And to disavow views that family and former friends regard as perfectly normal.

Edit yourself

For example, it'd be best not to mention that you still think Brexit was a good idea. Or that multiculturalism has failed and mass immigration is destroying your community. Or the rush to hit net zero before anyone else is a costly mistake. Or that if you're born with a penis it's most likely you're bloke. And that you're actually proud of Britain and its history, and still think it's the best country in the world.

Moreover, if you happen to be a devout Muslim, it would be very unwise to share your views on homosexuality.

Whether you like them or not, these opinions are commonplace in working class communities and, indeed, the world that exists beyond our bubble. But they'd be regarded as triggering in London's agencies.

And openly sharing them would get a new recruit cold-shouldered, reprimanded, or maybe "let go".

Incidentally, on September 13th, over 110,000 people, to whom most of the above views are regarded as quite normal, descended on London for their "Unite the Kingdom" rally. In the aftermath, the CEO of one large London agency felt it necessary to write to all staff members "about what this divisive agenda might mean for them and their families" and the concern that "these voices of hate still find a platform".[22]

The email did carry a vague hint that some staff members might possibly have joined the rally. But clearly the CEO had made no attempt to find out why they'd do that - or get their interpretation of the event itself. *The Guardian's* reporter, Helen Pidd, was more open-minded. She reported that, while there were some racists, "mostly these were 'ordinary people' with 'ordinary jobs' who 'care about our kids, who said time and again that they'd had enough". And coming to London like this was "the only place they could be heard."[23]

The CEO who wrote the email wasn't interested in listening. Her message had the assumptive, and even coercive, tone of someone at the very top who was speaking for everyone - and those who didn't feel included had better get with the programme.

We can be sure that her attitude was shared throughout adland's progressive Commissariat. And conclude that if they cannot bear to share their city streets with such folks for one day they won't stomach working with them week in, week out.

No, the people who marched on London are the kind of diverse thinkers that adland doesn't want around. And these barbarians must be kept well beyond the walls.

"Decentralised totalitarianism"

Few people will question that. Or dare to because of fear, insecurity and the pressure to conform.

Like those other activities rich in cultural capital, arts and academia, advertising's middle ranks have been hollowed out. What we're left with is a small number of well paid executives and a lot of cheap juniors.

The competition to grab and hold onto those top jobs is increasingly intense. And so is the pressure to keep quiet or actively promote policies that you know to be flawed.

Ben Cobley has observed that this works wherever diversity dogma takes root: "Conformity to the system has become a matter of self-interest as much as a political commitment. The carrot of favour and inclusion draws us in to conform while the stick of disfavour and exclusion draws us away from any doubts we may have."[24]

In effect, for over a decade, adland has taken on the characteristics of what sociologist Jonathan Haidt described as a "decentralised totalitarianism". There is no single dictator or clique controlling everybody through fear and force. Instead there's a willing submission to the groupthink that's policed by members of the group itself.

As Haidt says: "This thing that we call wokeness has elements that are totalitarian, but there's no person. There's no authority. So what you then have, when everybody can record everybody, when everybody can shame everybody, you get human behavior reacting as if you were in a totalitarian country, but yet there's no totalitarian."[25]

We need more extra-environmentalists

At its most intense, during peak purpose, compliance had become habitual. Many people in the industry were probably unaware this was even happening. They were too immersed in the milieu.

The great 1960s copywriter, Howard Gossage, said when attempting to explain the objective benefits of extra-environmental thought, "I don't know who it was that invented water, but it certainly wasn't a fish."[26]

And it took extra-environmental individuals to recognise the progressives' control of the industry and their fixation with social purpose. As I said on page xx, those who challenged the groupthink came from freelance or small independent agencies based out of London.

The rest of the industry seemed blind to the people and the things that matter most.

Be that the general public who should always be our focal point ... the importance of work that appeals to their self interest (not ours) and entertains them ... our clients, whose commercial success should be uppermost in our mind ... the need for people in a creative industry like ours to be able to think and speak freely ... the large sections of the population who've been excluded from the ads we produce and, perhaps most crucially, the ranks from which we are recruiting.

But while the progressive gaze has been fixed on its own righteous objectives, I'd argue that it has ignored the real moral failing that lies at the heart of the industry.

One which, although hidden in the plainest of sight, has been overlooked and unchallenged by our Left-leaning champions of social justice.

Indeed, while they have been ever alert to the plight of their favoured minorities, they've done nothing about the immiseration of the mass of people who work in UK advertising.

Which brings us full circle to the beginning of this book - and the passing of adland's golden age and the impact of that 20 year decline on the poor souls who labour in our industry today.

13
Or does the D stand for diversion?

We noted in Chapter 2 that things began to go wrong when adland surrendered to digital's time-saving and cost-cutting charms.

The financial crisis of 2008/09 only accelerated the transition and exacerbated the problem.

With no desks to work at, no time to do the work, no training on how it should be done and no protection from clients who wanted it cheaper and faster, agency staff morale started a downward spiral that has yet to bottom out.

Herded together like battery hens in some vast creative chicken coop, everyone knew something was wrong. But it took a survey by *Campaign US* in 2015 to point out just how bad things had become.

As the headline in *Forbes* magazine declared: "Madison Ave. blues: Why up to 70% of ad industry employees want to quit".

Apparently 37% of respondents rated morale as "low or dangerously low" while 42.5% said it was just "satisfactory".[1]

It seems nothing was done to arrest the decline because, 12 months later, the 2016 survey showed 47% felt morale was on the floor.[2]

The bosses are to blame

The findings prompted concerned industry comment from Europe to Asia. Everyone recognised the symptoms. And the cause. As the 2016 *Campaign US* survey revealed, 73% of those surveyed blamed bad management.

One respondent summed up how many were feeling: "Clients will always be clients. They can be bad, but rarely ever cause the true problems the industry is facing. We are doing it to ourselves. Specifically, the few rulers at the top of holding companies and their agencies are doing it to the rest of us. Starting to follow the golden rule of 'doing unto others as you'd have done to you' would be a step in the right direction. There's a complete lack of compassion from most in leadership positions. It is completely bizarre. Who raised these people?"[3]

Writing at the time, the Ad Contrarian Bob Hoffman wasn't surprised: "Under the 'leadership' of the financial sharpies, lawyers, and accountants who now control the agency holding companies, the advertising business has become a confused and chaotic mess.

"A business that valued ideas and creativity above all else is now a pig's breakfast of insufferable bullshit, dreadful jargon, stupid gimmicks, and amateur bumblers producing horrific crap.

"Morale has dropped because standards have dropped. Standards have dropped because the 'leaders' of our industry don't know what business they're in."[4]

Distract and mollify

Actually Bob was wrong about the last bit. The people at the very top knew exactly what business they were in. It centred on keeping personal control of the fiefdoms they managed.

And the best way to go about this was pretending they cared about making their employees' lives better.

Suddenly staff were being placated with dart boards, table footballs and basketball hoops. It was the workplace as playground, with shiatsu massage in the wellbeing hub that used to be the creative director's office.

That was the tactical response. But what of the long-term and lasting change that their staff were demanding?

Well, ask yourself: what's the best way to distract and mollify the vocal, influential members of an unhappy Left-leaning workforce?

That's right, tell them you share their zeal for social justice and "Change". And allow them to indulge their political vanity projects with their social purpose campaigns.

Then, in case that bandwagon hits the economic buffers, announce that you're also committing the organisation to the elimination of racial, ethnic and sexual discrimination - and the creation of a just and equitable company.

And hire serried ranks of HR and DE+I personnel to administer the new caring regime.

Nothing actually has to "Change". You stay at the top, while the rainbow coalition of workers that comes in through your target-hitting hiring policy have to graft just as hard in exactly the same conditions for less pay than the people they've replaced.

In other words, same vast creative chicken coop, just different coloured and gendered battery hens.

It was the answer to a problem, yes, but not the one uppermost in the workers' minds.

A lack of diversity wasn't the problem

At the time the *Campaign US* surveys came out, David Kirkpatrick, the contributing editor of *Marketing Drive* studied the reasons for the dissatisfaction and observed: "While diversity has been a major issue in the agency space, that didn't correlate with the study's findings on why employees had low morale."[5]

As we've seen, the finger was pointed directly at the bosses. But they baulked at addressing the systemic flaws in their own creaking agency models. Instead, they made a great play of addressing what progressives' saw as society's systemic prejudices.

Alas, signing off the expansion of DE+I teams with the brief to increase diversity and inclusion didn't make agency life any better.

In 2019, after questioning 576 ad agency personnel, the UK industry charity NABS declared that "The UK advertising and media industry is at risk of staff burnout as 63% say they're considering leaving the industry at some point due to work negatively impacting their wellbeing."[6]

When Covid 19 hit a year later, thousands actually did leave the workplace and have rarely bothered to go back. They are still drawing a salary, but their dislike of agency life means they'd prefer to work from home.

The response to BLM may have made things worse

After the murder of George Floyd, adland's fixation with Black Lives Matter and the need to atone for its prejudiced past pushed DE+I further to the front of agency life. But again its prominence did little to ameliorate the working condition of the majority of the industry's employees. Or change the miserable vibe.

Indeed, it could be argued that perceived favouritism for the "oppressed" groups poisoned workplace relations. Likewise such re-education sessions as mandatory unconscious bias training.

Numerous studies conclude that not only do they not work but they have the opposite effect of creating friction where little previously existed.[7]

Either way, the chronic unhappiness was evident in the increasing number of people quitting their jobs which, in 2022, saw a record churn rate of 32%.[8]

This Great Resignation put employees in the driving seat, and emboldened some to even start talking about organising advertising's workers.

Divide and rule

Indeed, 2021 had already seen the launch of the Creative Communication Workforce. Its founder, Sammi Ferhaoui, an account manager at Havas London explained optimistically: "The job market being as it is, it's a great opportunity because the balance of power is with workers more than it has been in forever, at least when it comes to advertising. But a lot of people are responding to it as individuals, by job shopping - just going for a slightly bigger salary or slightly better conditions. But if we want to achieve lasting change, we need to harness this opportunity collectively."[9]

This, of course, was precisely the kind of "Change" - and the solidarity it fostered - that leaders of adland's holding companies and biggest agencies wanted to avoid.

They realised, however, that the increasingly dissatisfied still needed to be appeased. So adland's leaders pointed to the Employee Resource Groups which were looking after the peculiar needs of BAME, women, LGBTQ+ and other favoured minorities.

According to McKinsey, who'd been enthusiastic proponents of DE+I initiatives: "The opportunity for organisations is clear: to position their ERG as sources of ideas and engines of change."[10]

But as Jennifer C. Pan countered in *Selling Social Justice*: "The real reason ERGs are ideal 'engines of change' for employers is that they don't threaten managerial power in any way and, at their most useful, even help stave off the threat of unionisation." She concluded that such workplace groups "theoretically operate for the benefit of workers but are organised and overseen by employers".[11]

As I pointed out on page 104 these top-down managed company unions divide the workforce into factions based on identity. And, in so doing, make it difficult to generate any sense of pan-worker solidarity. Worse still, the competition for favour can turn office life into one big circular firing squad with each group taking pot shots at the others.

The best way to break down prejudice

Likewise, such self-interest impedes any efforts to build an agency-wide *esprit de corps*. In fact, the nurturing of a grievance culture at the expense of a collective corporate culture is as big a barrier to fully functioning diversity and inclusion as any.

Sociologists Frank Dobbin and Alexandra Kalev have analysed over three decades of data on DE+I programmes collected from over 800 firms and have concluded that "having employees of different backgrounds work together towards a common goal appears to be a far more useful way of reducing bias in the workplace than subjecting them to tortuous training."[12]

Dobbin and Kalev are not alone. There are endless academic papers extolling the benefits of Intergroup Contact Theory and its variants i.e. the idea that people put aside differences when granted equal respect and status in their pursuit of a shared objective. Especially when that respect and status is earned through the talent each brings to the task.[13] Note here that the respect must be *earned* rather than *engineered* through some HR-led diversity drive.

In advertising's case, the shared objective should surely be the delivery of the most effective marketing and creative ideas to our clients.

And again, just as obviously, you accomplish that by aligning everyone in the agency to that objective, and developing and honing the skills they'll need to achieve it.

Refocussing attention

Progressive priorities can be a costly diversion. That's especially so when they are as open-endedly time-consuming as the fixation with DE+I.

I spoke to one CEO who encountered this situation upon assuming leadership of a top London agency.

"Initially I was struck by how much of the agency's energy was spent on diversity and HR related issues. What had been intended as an inclusive cultural strategy, had accidentally ended up creating quite a lot of division – and perhaps even more surprisingly, the conversation was so dominated by DE+I that we were no longer focused on what we do as a business, which is make brilliant work for our clients.

"I felt that we needed a cultural shift, to reintroduce a culture of excellence in what we do, in which of course we treat everyone equitably. And I think we've achieved that, so much so that it's now quite difficult to get people to complete the annual DE&I survey - not because they don't care about it, but because they don't feel we have so many issues to solve."

Not surprisingly, the agency's work has improved as a consequence. As have working relations.[14]

Breaking the class ceiling

There is, of course, a precedent for this.

Looking back to the 1960s and '70s, an historic, canyonesque class divide was bridged by some of our most brilliant advertising agencies.

The one that paved the way, Collett Dickenson Pearce, was the combustible combination of the posh, former wartime lieutenant colonel, John Pearce and curmudgeonly working class Yorkshireman, Colin Millward.

Perhaps its most famous alumni was the film director Alan Parker. His influence was explained by Paul Burke, another working class lad who's done very well in adland.

"His work changed advertising and wider culture, forever. The way he wrote and the people he cast were diverse, authentic and truly representative of the UK population."

In conversation, the two wondered if "a boy like Alan Parker could now go from an Islington council estate to a West End ad agency" and they concluded that "agencies' hiring criteria have been quietly but forcefully changed."

As Paul explained "However much they try to deny it, advertising agencies have a more discriminatory recruitment policy ... Despite the poverty of his upbringing, his gender and skin colour would now unfairly mark him out as 'privileged'. So the one privilege he did possess - his astonishing creative talent - might today go undiscovered."[15]

Doing great work is a force for good

Paul is right. And it's a tragedy because it was talent that broke the class barrier. Talent and a shared sense of excitement about working together to produce famous, ground-breaking work.

I talked about this to another product of the working class, art director Dave Dye.

The son of a Hoxton decorator, Dave now has more pencils to his name than a Crayola factory. He started as a trainee in the late 1980s and went on to work at such hot creative shops as Abbott Mead Vickers, Leagas Delaney and Mother.

At all of them, the determination to do great work transcended the class divide.

Dave recalls, ""One of the things that attracted me to advertising most was reading that the creative departments were meritocratic - the best idea won.

"I wouldn't be beaten by someone from a country estate just because I was from a council estate. I thought, if I work hard enough, I'll win.

"There seemed to be a general agreement on what was good and bad. And we put aside any differences just so long as we got the best ideas in front of the client. Everyone knew that the work was all that mattered."[16]

That was the focus then. But today it seems to have been replaced by an unedifying scramble for survival.

Another extra-environmentalist has the answer

Not surprisingly it took another independent maverick to pinpoint exactly where that problem - and the solution - lay.

In a 2022 podcast, Nils Leonard, the creative force behind the then independent Uncommon Creative Studio, explained that advertising had split between a few agencies that were in the creative business and a lot that were in the service industry.

"I think there's nothing in the middle. Businesses in the client service world are all about fees … deliveries … costs … efficiencies … spreadsheets … assets … and they're about content.

"And the result, of course, if you're in the client service industry, you can't move without your client's permission. You can't be dangerous or respected or arguably a partner because the word 'service' implies you work for them. If 90% of what you're offering them is 'yes' and "quicker' … and if what you're sought out for is not creativity, how can you be respected?

"Forgive me but the advertising industry is in the shit it made for itself when it decided not to stand for the magic power we have which is, of course, creativity."[17]

It sounds like Bob Hoffman's conclusion doesn't it? Remember how he described "A business that valued ideas and creativity above all else is now a pig's breakfast of insufferable bullshit, dreadful jargon, stupid gimmicks, and amateur bumblers producing horrific crap."[18]

Culpability at Cannes, D&AD and the IPA

Nils was speaking three years ago, and since then things have gone from bad to worse.

The cash-strapped major networks are quietly cutting back on the DE+I initiatives they so loudly trumpeted just a few years earlier.[19] But the false narrative of caring for the staff via various progressive policies whilst running the industry and the people who work in it into the ground still goes largely unchallenged.

And so, where once the agency was an exciting, enjoyable, inspiring place to hang out, it is now to be avoided. To someone of my age, who worked in an environment bursting with creative possibilities, the preference to WFH is akin to deciding to run away *from* the circus.

Alas, nowadays the circus has left town.

Recently nearly half (42%) of adland employees said they would consider looking for a new job if their employer required them to work in the office more than they currently do (which is an average of 2.6 days a week)[20]

Either way, whether you're at home or in the office, it seems adland has become sadland.

So much so that this May, David Eakins the art director and founder of well-being agency Happy Sapien, wrote an open letter to Cannes, D&AD and the IPA about them "rewarding the brilliance of the work while quietly accepting the suffering of those behind it".[21]

In effect he was urging the awards shows that had encouraged agencies to solve the problems of the world with their purpose campaigns to look closer to home. Their primary responsibility was to the long neglected workers under pressure to deliver.

At much the same time, and as if to reinforce the point, adland charity NABS revealed that it had received a record 5,200 calls for help with emotional support, stress, burnout and anxiety.[22]

The death knell for creatives

There's a lot to be anxious about. Because now advertising seems destined to serve not only its client masters but also the machinery brought to us by the all powerful Martech industry.

In June, Meta claimed that, within the next 18 months, its AI would create the entire ad – including imagery, video and text – and also target it to users in line with a client's budget.[23]

Obviously this would be the death knell for the creatives in the service-driven agencies. Their work life is characterised by a lack of training, non-existent briefs, impossible deadlines and clients who don't know what they want until they see the first iteration.

The result is often mediocre work at best. Or, in other words, precisely the kind of stuff that Meta promises to be able to generate in a fraction of the time and a fraction of the cost.

When the advertising world convened at Cannes a couple of weeks after Meta's announcement, there was a distinct sense that it "is in the shit it has made for itself".

Indeed, *Campaign's* editor-in-chief, Gideon Spanier, summed up the mood with his lead article: "'Change and fear' dominated at Cannes Lions as ad industry has less to roar about."[24]

Why isn't this fun anymore?

In the same week, *The Drum* ran Josh Clarricoats article: "Why isn't this fun any more?"

As he said: "None of us joined advertising because we wanted to dissect the minutiae of tech progress and how it impacts our jobs. None of us did it to become addicted to smartphones and only look in one place for creative answers. We came here because we thought we could get something more than money out of working.

"So what happens when it's not fun? When you don't have pride and enjoyment in what you create? Confidence, work, output, quality - they all drop ... As soon as moods dip and frustrations arise, it becomes more like a job, a chore that feeds into the work and the trust you have between client and agency."[25]

When I was reading this it put me in mind of a senior account person on a global account who once told me that "the work is just part of the tool kit of retention. Efficacy isn't a determinant of success. Just getting to the other side of the black hole with the client still on board is the aim."[26]

It's that kind of soul-destroying thinking that led Clarricoats to conclude: "Sure, there will always be people chasing the quickest route to the bottom line. But I'd wager most of you didn't get into this industry for that. You came for the thrill of the process - the joy of making, the pride in the craft, and the magic of bringing something unexpected to life."[27]

It's a cry for help from an industry desperate to reconnect with the very things that Messers Leonard and Hoffman were talking about.

Ideas, creativity, respect, pride in your work

And surely, even an emotional dyslexic could read adland's room and know this is where the solution to its main problem lies.

Finally the IPA twigged...

It's heartening to see that the IPA, the Advertising Association and ISBA have finally realised that hitting their identitarian diversity targets might not be the answer. Something else is wrong.

For the first time ever they used the 2025 All In Census to ask respondents if they actually enjoy working in advertising. A remarkable 78% said yes they do.

However, while they may well like the idea of advertising in general, they appear to despise the role they are being forced to play in particular. Because, across the industry, the crucial Employee Net Promoter Score was a dismal 6%.[28]

What does that mean? Well, when the highlights of the All In Census were presented to the media, it was glossed over as "lower than some other UK industries."[29]

However, according to the Academy to Innovate HR, a 6% eNPS score indicates that employees "are dissatisfied and unhappy with the company. They may actively criticise it and pose a risk to the organisation …. [and] may spread negative sentiments both internally and externally."[30]

...but got the wrong end of the stick

It's a shocking result and, if applied to a particular business, would be a savage indictment of senior management. Heads would surely roll.

But don't expect even a *mea culpa* from the people at the IPA, ISBA and the Advertising Association - or any other of adland's institutions who've presided over this mess.

Likewise the leaders of the holding companies for whom many of the disgruntled employees work.

Because, while it's encouraging to know that the All In Census is vaguely alert to the problem, it's disheartening to see that its probing into the causes goes no deeper than linking morale to the question of: "is advertising trusted" and whether it has "a positive impact on society?"

Again we see the argument being framed by the progressives' fixation with purpose and their interpretation of ethical behaviour.

It was a cue dutifully taken by *Creative Brief's* editorial director, Nicola Kemp who saw that data and concluded: "While advertising industry commentators have long scoffed at the importance of purpose in marketing, the universal truth remains that people who care about what they do are the ultimate competitive advantage."[31]

Once more it seems, the solution's social purpose, now what's the problem?

Start asking the right questions

But then again, pretty much every issue in the All In Census is seen from the progressive perspective – particularly when it comes to race, gender and ethnicity.

Yes, it is helpful to gather the statistics on discrimination against black, Asian, Muslim, women, trans, disabled etc. workers. Everybody wants to expunge that blight from the industry.

But when the figures tell us that discrimination would motivate 11% of people to shift jobs as opposed to the 71% who say "better opportunities/salary" it's clear we're looking in the wrong place if we're trying to understand the mood of the labour force.

Indeed, it seems that in our relentless focus on advertising's very own pyramid of oppression we've again lost sight of the things that matter most to the people in the industry.

In terms of understanding how to achieve a happier workforce and a thriving creative culture might it be better to also ask questions like:

Do you think you are paid enough for the hours you are working each week?

How much training do you get a month?

Are you encouraged/enabled to develop new skills?

Do you get sufficient guidance/support from your line managers?

Do you feel your C-level is committed to producing a product of which you and your colleagues can be proud?

Do you and your colleagues have a motivating professional mission/purpose?

Those findings would, I suggest, cast real light on why the respondents to the IPA's All In Census are "dissatisfied and unhappy with the company. They may actively criticise it and pose a risk to the organisation …. [and] may spread negative sentiments both internally and externally."

Readjusting the ideological lens

If adland fails to adjust its ideological lens in this way, it will never solve the plummeting morale crisis. Nor arrest advertising's drift to the margins of British business and cultural life.

Knocking out some YouTube films about the climate crisis might get a few dozen people a jolly in Cannes the third week of every June. But they won't improve the daily grind for the vast majority who work in our industry. Nor persuade clients to shift their budgets back to brand building campaigns and the creative agencies that produce them.

And those hyperserious, hectoring purpose ads certainly won't provide the entertaining and engaging work needed to rekindle the public's affection for what we do.

It's the same with that other *idée fixe*: the identitarian application of DE+I.

Increasing the number of young women amongst the ranks of those working 68 hours a week won't make those 68 hours any less arduous or boring. Nor will the recruitment of more BAME people to act as cannon fodder in the war of attrition that is contemporary agency life.

Sharing the shit jobs amongst the favoured groups is actually doing no one any favours. Especially as those jobs are precisely the ones that will be replaced by AI in 18 months' time.

Improving those shit jobs is surely the priority. Likewise enabling colleagues to express their talents rather than encouraging them to rehearse their grievances.

The aim should be to open our doors to people who might make us feel uncomfortable, and then give everyone a place they enjoy coming to; a sense of pride in their work, and crucially the chance to master their craft to a degree that cannot be matched by artificial intelligence.

Simultaneously we must convince the client that all this is commercially to their advantage.

That's what adland needs. Less of the progressive gaze. And much more creative vision. Or, as Nils Leonard said in his *cri de coeur* to his advertising colleagues, "Honestly, don't you just want to wake up and matter a little bit more?"[32]

If we don't allow that to happen, if we remain blind to the people and things that matter then a once vital, attractive, exciting and fun industry will continue its precipitous decline. And inevitably, one day in the none-too-distant, we'll be reading an AI-generated headline asking:

"Oh fuck, adland, what have you done?"

Notes

1: Vibe shift

1 "Jaguar has rebranded when it needed to revitalise", Mark Ritson, *Marketing Week*, 20 November, 2024

2 Jaguar Copy Nothing YouTube

3 "Hood Ornaments on Modern Jaguars: Look Before You Leap(er)?", Sherry Bryan, jaguarforums.com, 23 April, 2020

4 jaguarforums.com, 19 November, 2024

5 "Jaguar's woke ad shows just how out of touch companies are with consumers", Charles Gasparino, *New York Post,* November 30, 2024

6 "Jaguar's massive rebrand explained: what's all the fuss about?", Ollie Kew, *BBC Top Gear* 3, December 2024

7 John James, LinkedIn Post, 21 November, 2024

8 "Jaguar has rebranded when it needed to revitalise", Mark Ritson

9 John James, LinkedIn Post

10 "Jaguar's Santino Pietrosanti Speaking at the Attitude Awards", *YouTube Attitude Magazine*, 9 October, 2024

11 "Jaguar is not looking back on its radical rebrand ... quite literally: British car maker teases concept EV with NO REAR WINDOW", Rob Hull, *This is Money*, 22 November, 2024

12 Steve Harrison, *Can't Sell, Won't Sell: Advertising, Politics and Culture Wars,* London, 2022

13 John Gabriel, *X*, 19 November, 2024

14 "Why Bud Light Executive Alissa Heinerscheid's Words Are More Damaging Than People Think", *Martin Decoder, YouTube*, 7 September, 2023

15 "'Panic and rash decision-making': ex-Bud Light staff

on one of the biggest boycotts in US history", Owen Myers, *The Guardian,* 19 September, 2023

16 "Welcome to the 'mask-off' era", Jemima Kelly, *Financial Times*, 2 February, 2025

17 ibid.

18 "How Not to Plan: What Matters Most in 2025 - Les Binet and Sarah Carter", *The Uncensored CMO,* 8 January, 2025

2: Why adland embraced social purpose

1 "The Crisis of Creative Effectiveness", Peter Field, *The Institute of Practitioners in Advertising*, 2019

2 "Creative should be an adjective, not a noun", Richard Huntington, *Campaign*, 27 March, 2025

3 Seth Godin, *Permission Marketing: Turning Strangers into Friends and Friends into Customers,* New York, 1999

4 Rick Levine, Christopher Locke, Doc Searls and David Weinberger, *The Cluetrain Manifesto: The End of Business as Usual,* Cambridge, Mass., 1999

5 "Marketers lack influence in the boardroom", Jane Simms, *Campaign*, January 15, 2008

6 Professor Alan Tapp, Email exchange, 30 April, 2008

7 "UK newspaper ad revenues 'will fall by 21% in 2009'", Mark Sweney, *The Guardian*, 21 November, 2008

8 "Advertising in Recession: Long, Short or Dark", Peter Field, *Linkedin Blog*, January 2, 2021

9 "Creating shared value. how to reinvent capitalism—and unleash a wave of innovation and growth", Michael E Porter and Mark R Kramer, *Harvard Business Review*, Jan/Feb, 2011

10 Purpose of a Corporation Business Roundtable https://www.businessroundtable.org › ourcommitment

11 How organizing for sustainability can benefit the bottom line McKinsey & Company https://www.mckinsey.com › media › McKinsey

12 Research challenges relevance of popular ESG scoring ...University of California, Berkeley https://newsroom.haas.berkeley.edu › research › researc...

3: Why adland leans Left

1 "The Empathy Delusion", Andrew Tenzer and Ian Murray, Reach Solutions and house51, July, 2019

2 "Ian Murray – House 51: Uncovering the hard truths Part 1", *The Fuel Podcast with Keith Smith*, April 9, 2022

3 Jennifer C. Pan, *Selling Social Justice: Why the Rich Love Antiracism*, London and New York, 2025; Ben Cobley, *The Tribe: The Liberal-Left and the System of Diversity*, Exeter, 2018

4 Tomiwa Owolade, *This is not America: Why Black Lives in Britain Matter,* London, 2023

5 Andrew Tenzer and Ian Murray, "Why We Shouldn't Trust Our Gut Instincts", Trinity Mirror Solutions, 2018

6 "'All In' Census results: adland vows action on black, disabled and working-class talent", Kate Magee, *Campaign,* 29 July, 2021

7 "All In Census 2025: results show some progress but participation falters", Eszter Guibicz and Gideon Spanier, *Campaign,* 8 May, 2025

8 "Half of marketers say marketing qualification has 'advanced' their career" Charlotte Rogers, *Marketing Week,* 28 April, 2025; "Do you need a degree to work in media and advertising?" Ella Sagar, *The Media Leader,* 1 August, 2020

9 "Do you need a degree to work in media and advertising?", Ella Sagar

10 "Killing the elephant in the diversity room - social class". Lisa Thpmpson, *IPA Blog,* 14 May, 2020

11 "Londoncentric adland: 85% of staff at big six agency groups are based in capital", Gideon Spanier, *Campaign*, October 14, 2020

12 "VCCP Stoke Academy: the young talent scheme putting its money where its mouth is", Conor Nichols, *Creative Salon,* 25 July, 2024

13 "All In, UK Advertising Census 2025", *Institute Practitioners in Advertising*. May, 2025

14 "How Britain voted in the 2024 general election", Adam McDonnell, *YouGov*, July 8, 2024

15 "Here's what you told us about how you're intending to vote in today's general election." Editorial Team, *The Drum,* July 4, 2024.

16 "Wages worth less than in 2008", *Labour Research Department*, 1 May, 2024

17 "Home Ownership and the UK Mortgage Market: An International Review", *Tony Blair Institute for Global Change*, 11 April, 2022

18 "How much have UK property prices increased over the past 50 years?", Rommel Lontayeo, *Mortgage Introducer*, 14 June, 2022

19 "UK House Price Index April 2025", *HM Land Registry*, 18 June, 2025

20 "How Britain voted in the 2024 general election", Adam McDonnell, *YouGov*, July 8, 2024

21 ibid.

22 "Freedom of speech in higher education", *Report to the Office of Students by YouGov,* 16 June, 2025

23 "The Times Higher Education academic freedom survey 2024", *Times Higher Education*, Paul Jump, 5 December, 2024

24 Matt Goodwin, *Bad Education: Why Our Universities Are Broken and How We Can Fix Them*, London, 2024

25 "Cardiff University runs compulsory 'EDI Awareness Module' for first-year students", *Committee for Academic Freedom*, 1 March, 2025

26 "Agency sizes, structures, departments and salaries", *The Institute of Practitioners in Advertising*, 23 June, 2025

27 "Thorstein Veblen's Theory of the Leisure Class - A Status Update", Rob Henderson, *Rob Henderson's Newsletter*, January 29, 2023

28 ibid.

29 "Always Pippa 2021" UK, YouTube

30 "The Global Wellness Economy Reaches a New Peak of $6.3 Trillion—And Is Forecast to Hit $9 Trillion by 2028", *Global Wellness Institute*, 5 November, 2024

31 Obesity Profile: short statistical commentary May 2024 - GOV.UK/GOV.UKhttps://www.gov.uk › government › statistics › obesity-...

32 "The Empathy Delusion", Andrew Tenzer and Ian Murray, Reach Solutions and house51, July, 2019

33 Jonathan Haidt, *The Righteous Mind: Why Good People are Divided by Politics and Religion*, (London, 2012); "The Moral Mind: Researcher blazes the way in our understanding of moral sensibilities", Harrison Tasoff, *The Current,* University of Santa Barbara, 20 August, 2019.

34 Moral Foundation Theory, moralfoundation.org.
35 Vicki Maguire, "Has adland lost sight of its purpose",
   Campaign, March 10, 2021

4: Advertising and activism

1 "Power 100: Brand purpose shines through out of the
   gloom", Gemma Charles, *Campaign*, 13 October,
   2020
2 *Campaign*, December 2020/January 2021
3 "The Year Ahead", *Campaign*, December 2020/January
   2021
4 "Change has to come with empathy. Fierce,
   uncompromising empathy", Lucy Jameson,
   Campaign, December 2020/January 2021
5 "Creativity is the only way we will survive", Sheryl
   Marjoram, *Campaign*, December 2020/January 2021
6 "Technology doesn't solve problems by itself"', Fura
   Johannesdottir, *Campaign*, December 2020/January
   2021
7 "In 2021, Work-From-Home-forever realties will set in."
   Emma Chui, *Campaign*, December 2020/January 2021
8 "Anti-Trump protests continue across US as 10,000
   march in New York", Edward Helmore, *The
   Guardian*, 12 November, 2016
9 "Captivating Gen Z's attention is critical", Peter
   Semple, *Campaign*, Winter, 2021/22
10 "The climate emergency is a huge marketing
   opportunity", Katie Mackay-Sinclair, *Campaign*,
   Winter, 2021/22
11 "We must deliver societal value", Lori Meakin,
   Campaign, Winter, 2021/22

12 "Frustration is good. It is petrol for innovation", Natalie Graeme, *Campaign*, Winter, 2021/22

13 "In-platforming moments are shaping offline behaviours", Ella Dolphin, *Campaign*, Winter, 2021/22

14 "Stop playing defence. It's time to move forward with confidence", Tammy Einev, *Campaign*, Winter, 2021/22

15 "We need to get closer to customers", Aline Santos, *Campaign*, Winter, 2021/22

16 Thomas Sowell, *The Vision of the Anointed: Self-Congratulation as the Basis for Social Policy*, New York, 1995

17 "Unleashing Creativity Against Adversity", Suzy Bashford, *Campaign*, December 2020/January 2021

18 "Episode 27:Tim Lindsay", Ben Kay*, If this is a blog then what's Christmas?"* 12 November, 2020

19 ibid.

20 "How Should Brands Navigate the Culture War?", *Little Black Book,* 28 March, 2023

21 ibid.

22 ibid.

23 ibid.

24 "The lives of others. To find a way in, we must find the way out of our own", Martin Weigel, *Canalside View,* 8 March, 2021

25 "WPP's Mark Read on ESG and turning down clients who don't 'do the right thing'", Gideon Spanier, *Campaign*, July 6, 2021

26 "Purpose is the Future of Business", Aline Santos, *effie*

27 "Unilever CEO Alan Jope: We'll dispose of brands that don't stand for something", Stephen Lepitak, *The Drum,* 19 June, 2019

28 Mark Borkowski, LinkedIn post, February, 2025

29 "Stop propping up brand purpose with contrived data and hypocrisy", Mark Ritson, *Marketing Week,* 25 July, 2018

30 "Samsung Europe CMO on why it's time for marketing to mature", Benjamin Braun, *The Drum,* 16 Sept, 2020

31 "Mastercard's CMO on the existential threat facing marketers", Kendra Barnett, *The Drum,* 27 September, 2021

5: Post-purpose

1 "Bank Rate Increased to 5.25% - August 2023", *The Bank of England*, 3 August, 2023

2 "UK inflation jumps to 11.1% on back of energy and food price rises", Larry Elliot, *The Guardian*, 16 November, 2022

3 "Unilever's CMO of ice cream on prioritising 'product superiority' over purpose", Niamh Carroll, *Marketing Week*, 23 November, 2022

4 ibid.

5 ibid.

6 "Unilever hails 'brand power' amid pledge to 'take the lead' on price" Niamh Caroll, *Marketing Week*, 27 Oct 2022

7 Magnum | Stick to the original (full version) YouTube Magnum 3 Jan 2024

8 "P&G's Marc Pritchard: 'The industry has gone too far with purpose marketing'", Jennifer Faull, *The Drum*, 30 June, 2022

9 "Here's a purpose-based initiative, Ben Kay, *If this is a blog then what's Christmas?,* 26 June, 2022

10 "P&G finance chief: Product 'superiority' has shielded brands from private label impact", Niamh Carroll, *Marketing Week*, 7 December, 2023

11 Conversation with Justin Tindall, 23 April, 2021

12 "Purpose work has dominated Cannes. Creatives are eying a shift toward business results and humor", James Fleming, *Adweek*, June 12, 2023

13 "Cannes Lions: President Clinton calls on ad agencies to inspire social change", Stephen Lepitak, *The Drum*, June 22, 2012

14 "Spike Lee reminds adland creatives: your priority is to 'sell shit, by hook or by crook'", Nicola Merrifield, *Campaign*, June 26, 2023

15 Bob Hoffman, Email exchange, 16 April, 2022

16 *Why Does the Pedlar Sing? What Creativity Really Means in Advertising,* Paul Feldwick, Leicester, 2021

17 System1 Group https://system1group.com

18 "Does creativity still drive business?", Gurjit Degun, *Campaign*, 26 September, 2022

19 *Lemon. How the Advertising Brain Turned Sour*, Orlando Wood, London, 2019; *Look Out*, Orlando Wood, London, 2021

20 *The Road to Hell: How Purposeful Business Leads to Bad Marketing and a Worse World. And How Human Creativity is the Way Out*, Nick Asbury, Gloucester, 2024

21 Nick Asbury, email exchange, 12 April, 2025

6: The long march through adland's institutions

1 "Episode 27:Tim Lindsay", Ben Kay, *If this is a blog then what's Christmas?",* 12 November, 2020

2 ibid.

3 "D&AD announces appointment of Patrick Burgoyne as chief executive", *Little Black Book*, 26 September, 2019

4 "Do creative agencies need to work on their purpose?" Patrick Burgoyne, *Creative Review,* August, 2019

5 URGE Collective https://www.urgecollective.com

6 "Ben Terrett declines D&AD presidency citing lack of diversity", Jennifer Hain, *Dezeen*, 12 October, 2020

7 "D&AD's new president: 'The world is burning and life's not always fair'", Emmet McGonagle, *Campaign*, 8 October, 2020

8 D&AD https://www.dandad.org › d-ad-creative-inspiration-din...... Protest, Typography, and the Fight for Justice – Tré Seals on a practice rooted in purpose.

9 "How do we solve a problem like ... attracting bright young talent", Sam Bradley, *The Drum*, 3 November, 2020

10 "Pentagram partner Naresh Ramchandani named D&AD President for 20/21", Bill Langsworthy, *Mojo Nation*, 19 October, 2020

11 Message from 2021 President Naresh Ramchandani D&AD https://www.dandad.org › annual › presidents-letter-2021

12 Naresh Ramchandani recalls the ethical and commercial ...D&AD https://www.dandad.org › annual › editorial › book-of-.

13 "Here's a purpose-based initiative, Ben Kay, *If this is a blog then what's Christmas?*, 26 June, 2022

14 Ben Kay, LinkedIn post, June 2022

15 "D&AD Challenges the Creative Industry to 'MAKE. CHANGE.' with Return of in-Person Festival", *Little Black Book*, 24 April, 2023

16 A Letter from D&AD CEO Jo Jackson … D&AD
https://www.dandad.org › annual › 2023

17 "Adlanders work long hours because clients don't
pay their agencies enough money", Tim Lindsay,
Campaign, 13 May, 2021

18 "D&AD announces its 2024 award winners", Rebecca
Fulleylove, *Creative Review,* 23 May, 2023

19 ibid.

20 Nick Asbury, LinkedIn post, June 2024

21 "D&AD names Kwame Taylor-Hayford as next
president", Ida Axling, Campaign, 3 October, 2024

22 ibid.

23 D&AD - 305992 - Charity Commission GOV.UK
https://register-of-charities.charitycommission.gov.uk

24 "D&AD Awards 2025: who won what?" Katy Cowan,
Creative Boom, 22 May, 2025

25 ibid.

27 THE IPA ARCHIVE The Institute of Practitioners in
Advertising The National Archives
https://discovery.nationalarchives.gov.uk › GB 03

28 "Effective on Purpose: An Evidence-Based Approach
to Brand Purpose", Carlos Grande, *Institute of
Practitioners in Advertising,* 2021

29 "The IPA Effectiveness Awards are not 'watering
down their criteria'", Harjot Singh, *Campaign*, 17
February, 2022

30 ibid.

31 "Peter Field and IPA: Purpose campaigns drive
customer acquisition and market share", Sam
Bradley, *The Drum*, 11 October, 2021

32 "Well-executed purposeful ads are 'incredibly
effective', IPA research shows", Nicola Merrifield,
Campaign, 12 October, 2021

33 "Brand purpose skeptics take a 'very different story'

from Peter Field's IPA study", John McCarthy, *The Drum*, 14 October 2021

34 "Hmmm, Danone", Nick Asbury, *Substack Thoughts on Writing*, 25 October, 2021

35 "Karen Martin pledges to put creativity at heart of IPA in inaugural speech", Alessandra Scotto di Santolo, *Campaign*, 31 March, 2025

36 "IPA President Karen Martin unveils agenda to revitalise UK advertising", *Institute of Practitioners in Advertising*, 31 March, 2025

37 Debating Group https://www.debatinggroup.co.uk › 2024/11 › dg.. The anti-woke agenda is fuelling creativity

38 ibid.

39 "Advertising Association names Publicis Groupe UK chief as new chair", Nicola Merrifield, *Campaign*, 7 June, 2022

40 Tim Lindsay, LinkedIn post, 12 May, 2021

41 Creative Industries 2025 Salary CensusMajor Players https://www.majorplayers.co.uk › the-creative-industries.

42 ibid.

Part 2

7: Equity or enmity?

1 "HR Britain: how human resources captured the nation", Pamela Dow, *The New Statesman*, 27 November, 2024

2 ibid.

3 ibid.

4 "HR directors outpaced peers in salary growth in the past year, research finds", Mahalia Mayne, *People Management*, 4 April, 2025

5 The rise of the Chief HR Officer KPMG https://assets.kpmg.com › dam › pdf › 2017/03

6 Conversation, Source undisclosed, 16 April, 2025

7 Ash Sarkar, *Minority Rule: Adventures in the Culture War*, London, 2025

8 Report on the Inclusion at Work Panel's recommendations ...GOV.UK https://www.gov.uk › government › publications › repo...

9 "UK graduates facing worst job market since 2018 amid rise of AI, says Indeed", Lauren Almeida, *The Guardian,* 25 June, 2025

10 Michael Foucault, *The Archaeology of Knowledge: And the Discourse on Language*, trans: A.M. Sheridan Smith, London 1972; *The Order of Things: An Archaeology of the Human Sciences,* London 2002, Jacque Derrida, *Of Grammatology*, trans: Gayatari Chakravorty Spivak, Baltimore 1976; Jean Francois Lyotard, *The Postmodern Condition: A Report on Knowledge*, Manchester, 1991

11 Derrick Bell, *Faces at the Bottom of the Well: The Permanence of Racism*, New York, 1992; Kimberle

Crenshaw, Neil Gotanda, Garry Peller, Kendall Thomas, *Critical Race Theory: The Key Writings that Formed the Movement*, New York, 1996; Judith Butler: *Gender Trouble: Feminism and the Subversion of Identity*, Abingdon, 2006; White Privilege: Unpacking the Invisible Knapsack UW Homepage https://admin.artsci.washington.edu › sites › files; Andrew Doyle, *The New Puritans: How the Religion of Social Justice Captured the Western World*, London, 2023;

12 Helen Pluckrose and James Lindsay, *Cynical Theories: How Activist Scholarship Made Everything About Race, Gender, and Identity - and Why This Harms Everybody,* Croydon, 2021: Jennifer C Pan, *Selling Social Justice: Why the Rich Love Antiracism*, New York 2025; Tomiwa Owolade, *This is not America: Why Black Lives in Britain Matter*, London, 2023

13 Ben Cobley, *The Tribe: The Liberal Left and the System of Diversity*, Exeter, 2018

14 Ibram X. Kendi, Penguin Books UK https://www.penguin.co.uk › authors › ibram-x-kendi

15 Gail Parminter, email exchanges, 11 March, 2025

16 Dave Trott, "The politics of humiliation", *Campaign,* 8 October, 2020

17 "Repositioning Diversity as a Strategic Intent", Helena Morrissey, LinkedIn, 17 January, 2025

18 "Is DEI Doomed? An HR Director Speaks (Ft Neil Morrison)" *This Isn't Working.* 18 September, 2024; "HR 's Critics Turn up the Heat (Ft, Levi Pay)" *This Isn't Working,* 17 December, 2024

19 BBC senior managers who tick 'diversity' boxes paid more, ...MSN http://www.msn.com › en-gb › money › other › bbc-seni...

20 "Civil servants in Scotland 'more likely to be promoted if they're gay'", Simon Johnson and Marc Macaskill, *Daily Telegraph*, 20 March, 2025

21 Conversation, Source undisclosed, 5 July, 2025

22 "This advertising boss thinks women should make up 40% of senior positions in the ad industry", Lare O'Reilly, *Business Insider,* 14 January, 2016

23 School Reports 2025: A to Z Campaign https://www.campaignlive.co.uk › article › school-repor...

8: Positive discrimination in adland?

1 "Adland's gender pay gap drops below national average for first time", Shauna Lewis and Elena Lewis, *Campaign,* 19 May, 2025

2 "ALL IN UK Advertising Census", 2025 Key Findings, Advertising Association, ISBA, IPA

3 The gender pay gap is not a myth, it's math - Of Boys and Men Richard V Reeves | Substack https://ofboysandmen.substack.com › comments

4 Opinion | The Gender Pay Gap Is a Culture Problem The New York Times https://www.nytimes.com › 2024/05/22 › gender-pay-gap

5 "Upper-class romance: homogamy at the apex of the class structure", Maren Toft & Vegard Jarness, *European Societies,* Volume 3, 2021.

6 "Wacl campaign accelerates push to smash 50% women CEO ceiling", Ben Bold, *Campaign*, 17 April, 2023

7 "How a 'new generation of female leadership' is breaking down barriers", Jennifer Small, *Campaign*, 22 October, 2024

8 "Adland's gender pay gap is widening. Is this the unorthodox fix?", Paul Burke, *The Drum*, 4 April, 2025

9 Gen Z: Trends, Truth and Trust Channel 4 https://assets-corporate.channel4.com › _flysystem

10 Lost Boys The Centre for Social Justice https://www.centreforsocialjustice.org.uk › ... › CSJ

11 "ALL IN UK Advertising Census", 2025 Key Findings

12 "School Reports 2025: The 'broken pipeline' of diverse leadership", Jennifer Small, *Campaign*, 19 March, 2025

13 2024 IPA Agency Census, *Institute of Practitioners in Advertising*

14 "Campaign faces to watch 2022, Matt Barker, *Campaign;* "Campaign faces to watch 2023, Matt Barker, *Campaign;* "Campaign faces to watch 2024" Matt Barker, *Campaign*

15 "Faces to Watch 2024: Polly Norkett", Polly Norkett, *Campaign*, 17 September, 2024

16 "School Reports 2025: The 'broken pipeline' of diverse leadership", Jennifer Small

17 2024 IPA Agency Census, *Institute of Practitioners in Advertising*

18 ibid.

19 UK Creative Industries Census 2023, *Major Players, London and Manchester*

20 UK Creative Industries Census 2025, *Major Players, London and Manchester*

21 ibid.

22 UK Creative Industries Census, 2024, *Major Players, London and Manchester*

23 "ALL IN UK Advertising Census", 2025 Key Findings

24 Sexual orientation, UK: 2023 Office for National

Statistics https://www.ons.gov.uk › bulletins › sexualidentityuk

25 "New data reveals most popular occupations of lesbian, gay and bisexual people", Ian Jones, *Independent*, 26 October, 2023

26 "School Reports 2025: The 'broken pipeline' of diverse leadership", Jennifer Small

27 Ethnicity facts and figures – GOV.UK GOV.UK https://www.ethnicity-facts-figures.service.gov.uk

28 Trust for London https://trustforlondon.org.uk › data › geography-popul.

29 "How imposter syndrome and racism overlap", Bina Kandola, *HR*, 28 August, 2029

30 "Killing the elephant in the diversity room - social class". Lisa Thompson, *IPA Blog,* 14 May, 2020

31 Report on the Inclusion at Work Panel's recommendations ...GOV.UK https://www.gov.uk › government › publications › repo...

32 "Where DEI went wrong—and what must happen next", Aparna Rae, *Forbes*, 12 March, 2025

33 How do Britons define social class? YouGov /Research https://yougov.co.uk › society › articles › 51105-how-do...

34 "All In Census reveals Adland's hybrid working stalemate", Nicola Kemp, *Creative Brief,* 8 May, 2025

9: Why there are so many (not very) black faces on your screens

1 George Floyd: The murder that drove America to the brink https://www.bbc.co.uk › world-us-canada-56825822

2 "BAME representation drops at UK agencies, IPA Census reveals", Simon Gwynn, *Campaign*, 29 April, 2020

3 "Adland open letter calls for solidarity and action after death of George Floyd", Brittaney Kiefer, *Campaign,* 3 June, 2020

4 "Time to ditch the 'race-washing' in ads" Dino Myers-Lamptey, *Campaign*, 27 October, 2021

5 Research into Racial and Ethnic Stereotyping in Advertising, Rob Ellis and Dino Myers-Lamptey, *Advertising Standards Authority, prepared by COG Research, May, 2022*

6 "We Were There: How Black Culture, Resistance and Community Shaped Modern Britain", Lanre Bakare, London, 2025

7 "The Quiet Revival: A new generation leading church growth", Emma Lawson, *tearfund*, 16 April, 2025

8 "UK Black churches thrive like never before", *Renewal Journal*, 24 May, 2022

9 "Population of England and Wales", *GOVUK Ethnicity Facts and Figures* 22 December, 2022

10 "Advertising, gender, diversity, brands and charity: 5 interesting stats to start the week", Niamh Carroll, *The Drum*, 11 March, 2024

11 "New study reveals 77% of Black British individuals feel more represented by ad campaigns than a decade ago", *More About Advertising,* 28 September, 2023

12 Representation in Advertising Tracker, *ISBA*, March 2024

13 ibid.

14 "Mirror on the industry": How diverse and inclusive is TV advertising in 2019?", *Channel 4 Insight and YouGov*, 2018

15 ibid.

16 Diamond: The Seventh Cut, *Creative Diversity Network*, 12 September 2024

17 "Brands could learn a lot about South Asian representation from this flour ad", Sadia Siddiqui, *The Drum,* 5 October, 2023

18 "British Asian representation in ads: 'You can't just show a woman in a hijab and call it a day', Ellen Ormesher, *The Drum*, 9 December, 2021

19 Brands need to catch up - Mud Orange Mud Orange https://www.mudorange.com › insights › brands-need-t...

20 Representation in Advertising Tracker, *ISBA,* March 2024

21 "British East and Southeast Asian Representation in UK TV: A Deepening Crisis", *Resonate,* 14 June, 2025

22 "The extraordinary success of the British-Chinese community is a lesson to us all", Rakib Ehsan, *CapX,* 1 February, 2022

23 *Beyond Grievance: What the Left Gets Wrong About Ethnic Minorities*, Rakib Ehsan, London, 2023

24 Representation in Advertising Tracker, *ISBA*, March 2024

25 "Working class audiences want the BBC to take more risks when producing new programmes", *Ofcom,* 30 November 2023

26 "Writer calls for more working-class people in TV", Steven McKintosh, *BBC News*, 21 August, 2024

27 ibid.

28 "Mirror on the Industry audit reveals all," *Channel 4 News,* 30 September, 2025

29 https://youtu.be/x6VyvxqjPXA?si=HWEzyRoNk1tVxq

30 Coronation Street, 15 September, 2025–19 September, 2025

31 "Regional Ethnic Diversity", GOV.UK , 22 December, 2022

32 "How life has changed in Blackpool: Census 2021", Office of National Statistics, 19 January, 2023

33 Healthy Life Expectancy, Lancashire County Council

34 "Population by ethnicity and change 2011-21", Lancashire County Council

35 "Regional ethnic diversity", GOV.UK, 22 December 2022

36 Angus (Council Area, United Kingdom) City Population https://citypopulation.de › wards › S12000041__angus

37 "Diversity in Britain is more complicated than it seems", Ben Walker, *The New Statesman*, 16 March, 2022

38 How life has changed in Blackburn with Darwen: Census ...Office for National Statistics https://www.ons.gov.uk › censusareachanges

39 "Increased Attention to Racial Inequality Alters Consumer Responses to Black Actor Representation in TV Advertising", Koen Pauels and Yakov Bart, *Northeastern University D'Amore-McKim School of Business*, 2 June, 2023

40 "Racial diversity in TV commercials can backfire if not seen as genuine, new study finds", Alëna Kuzub, *Northeastern Global News,* 15 June, 2023

41 "Sentencing guidelines ditched after 'two-tier' row", Henry Jeffman and Joshua Nevett, *BBC News*, 31 March, 2025

41 "Teachers will be trained to challenge 'whiteness' in schools'", Craig Simpson, *The Telegraph*, 25 August, 2024

42 "No 10 condemns London theatre for hosting Black Out nights", Peter Walker, *The Guardian*, 29 February 2024

43 "'Woke' Labour council faces claims it tells staff to take 'white privilege' test - and they are marked down if they shop at Waitrose or M&S, drive a new car or are a white male", Robert Folker, *Daily Mail*, 2 April, 2025

44 "Shakespeare's birthplace trust to 'decolonise' collection amid claims of promoting 'white supremacy'" Sami Quadri, *Evening Standard,* 16 March, 2025

45 "One in three BBC journalism scheme trainees are white Britons", Jacob Freedland, *The Telegraph*, 27 April, 2025

46 "Baroness Casey's audit of group-based child sexual exploitation and abuse", Home Office and Rt. Hon. Yvette Cooper, GOV.UK, 16 June, 2025

47 "British countryside is a 'racist and colonial' white space, wildlife charities claim", Emma Soteriou, *LBC*, 8 February, 2025

48 "Tories to force Labour to choose rights of residents over migrants", Charles Hymas, *The Telegraph*, 31 August, 2025

49 Paul Embery, *Despised: Why the Modern Left Loathes the Working Class*, Cambridge, 2021

50 "Girl in union flag dress barred from giving speech on school's 'culture day'", Sally Weale, *The Guardian,* 15 July, 2025

51 Deborah Mattinson, *Beyond the Red Wall: Why Labour Lost, How the Conservatives Won and What Will Happen Next*, London 2020

10: Diversity and inclusion or division and intrusion?

1 "Starmer's 'thought police' turning off working class voters, says, Labour peer", Amy Gibbons, *The Telegraph,* 7 May 2025
2 Robin DiAngelo *White Fragility: Why It's So Hard for White People to Talk About Racism,* Boston, 2019
3 Ash Sarkar, *Minority Rule: Adventures in the Culture War*, London, 2025
4 Research into Racial and Ethnic Stereotyping in Advertising, Rob Ellis and Dino Myers-Lamptey, *Advertising Standards Authority, prepared by COG Research, May, 2022*
5 "Heinz apologises after ad featuring black family sparks anger online", Neha Gohil, *The Guardian*, 6 October, 2024
6 "Heinz faces backlash over negative stereotypes in ad", Evie Barrett, *Campaign*, 7 October, 2024
7 "When a Heinz advert features racist stereotypes to sell pasta sauce, it's vital to speak out. So I did", Nels Abbey, *The Guardian*, 8 October, 2024
8 "The false narrative of BAME vs white", *The Spectator*, 31 March, 2021
9 ibid.
10 "'National disgrace' so many pupils are 'written off'", says Phillipson, *TES Magazine*, 11 August, 2025
11 Miriam Cates, *X*, 11 August, 2025
12 "The demonisation of the white working class boys is the real 'national disgrace'", Toby Young, *The Telegraph*, 12 August, 2025
13 "Do children in two-parent families do better?", Branwen Jeffreys, *BBC News*, 12 August 2019

14 "Two Nations: The State of Poverty in the UK," *Centre for Social Justice,* December, 2023

15 "Nigel Farage exclusive: 'Advertising? I might fancy it myself one day'", Paul Simpson, *Campaign*, July 17, 2019

16 ibid.

17 "Why that Nigel Farage feature was a mistake", Andy Nairn, *Campaign*, 19 July, 2019

18 "Addressing our Nigel Farage coverage", Claire Beale, *Campaign,* 18 July, 2019

19 More in Common UK, *Tracking Public Opinion,* 17-20th October, 2025; *More in Common UK, September MRP,* 28 September, 2025

20 "British Politics - Next Prime Minister after Keir Starmer Betting Odds", *Odds Checker*, 29 August, 2025

21 Repressive Tolerance (full text) Marcuse.org https://www.marcuse.org › herbert › publications › 1965

22 "The Sun, Daily Mail and Express advertisers targeted in 'Stop Funding Hate' campaign", Louise Ridley, *Huffpost,* 16 August, 2016

23 "Inside The Daily Mail and Stop Funding Hate's unexpected brand safety truce", Chris Sutcliffe, *The Drum*, 6 July, 2021

24 "The Spectator, the Co-op and cancel culture – a cautionary tale", Fraser Nelson, *The Spectator*, 24 September, 2020

25 ibid.

26 "The strange boycott of GB News", Tom Slater, *The Spectator*, 15 June, 2021

27 "Andrew Neil challenges brands and agencies to debate GB News boycott on air", Sean Hargrave, *Campaign*, 21 June, 2021

28 Undisclosed source, Email exchange, 26 September 2021, Undisclosed source, Email exchange, 15 October, 2021

29 "WPP agency backed out of relationship with GB News", Daniel Farey-Jones, *Campaign,* 2 August, 2023

30 "GB News advertising boycott: the media planner's perspective", James Wilde, *Campaign*, 10 August, 2021

31 Angelos Frangopoulos, Conversations, 12 September, 2025

32 ibid.

33 THE OFCOM BROADCASTING CODE www.ofcom.org.uk https://www.ofcom.org.uk › legacy-codes › ofco...

34 Conversation with Angelos Frangopoulos

35 "GB News advertising boycott: the media planner's perspective", James Wilde

36 "GB News ratings milestone", Josh, *beBROADCAST,* 11 August, 2025; "GB News dealt figures blow after claiming to be number one news channel", Rebecca Jones, *Daily Express,* 13 August, 2025

37 "I thought, 'Wow, I could probably do this': A Listers on their favourite TV ads of all time", Eszeter Gurbicz, *Campaign,* 21 May, 2025

38 Employment Tribunals Judgment Between Claimants Respondents: Mr C Bayfield Mr C Jenner, v Wunderman Thompson (UK) Limited (1) Mr L Peon (2) Ms E Hoyle (3). Held at London Central on 8-12, 15-19 & 22-26 February 2021

39 ibid.

40 ibid.

41 ibid.

42 "Ad men sacked to improve gender pay gap win sex

discrimination claim", Rupert Neate, *The Guardian*, 23 July, 2021

43 ibid.

44 ibid.

45 "EXCLUSIVE: 'If I'd been a young, black, gay woman I'd have been ok': Two men at ad agency JWT win sex discrimination case after gay female director vowed to 'obliterate' Mad Men reputation of being full of 'white, straight men'", Alyssa Guzman, Andrew Young, Tom Pyman, *Daily Mail*, 10 December, 2021

46 ibid.

47 Middle-aged white men win sexism case after company addressed gender pay gap, Tom Williams, *Metro,* 23 July 2021

48 "EXCLUSIVE: 'If I'd been a young, black, gay woman I'd have been ok': Two men at ad agency JWT win sex discrimination case after gay female director vowed to 'obliterate' Mad Men reputation of being full of 'white, straight men'", Alyssa Guzman, Andrew Young, Tom Pyman

49 Email exchange, Source undisclosed

50 Tango - St. George (1997, UK) YouTube · The Hall of Advertising 10.8K+ views · 10 years ago

51 "St George's cross 'intimidating', council says", Patrick Hughes, BBC, 22 August, 2025; "Brighton council speaks out after St George's flags removed", *The Argos*, 29 August, 2025

52 "Patriot games, pop and purple prose", Peter York, *The Independent,* 26 0ctober, 1996

53 Dave Trott, LinkedIn post

54 "What's the best business advice you've ever been given?" Sir John Hegarty, LinkedIn post

55 Elle M Drew, Instagram, August 2025

56 "Born in the USA: Is American Eagle really using

whiteness to sell jeans?", Chloe MacDonnell, *The Guardian*, 1 August, 2025

57 "Sydney Sweeney has just sent this American stock soaring", Chris Price, *The Telegraph*, 24 July, 2025

58 Sydney Sweeney Has Great (American Eagle) Jeans American Eagle https://investors.ae.com › press-releases › news-detail

59 *D&AD. The Copy Book: How Some of the Best Advertising Writers in the World Write their Advertising*, London 2018

60 Undisclosed source, Conversation, 1 March, 2025

61 Rory Sutherland, email exchange, 14 April, 2021

62 "We are experiencing an unusually high volume of bureaucracy", Rory Sutherland, *The Spectator*, 1 July, 2023

63 Undisclosed source, Conversation, 7 April, 2025

64 Undisclosed source, Conversation, 23 June, 2025

65 LinkedIn message, Source undisclosed

11: Doubling down on DE+I

1 "Trump's war on 'woke': Both sides say the issue is further dividing the country", Bill Hutchinson, *abc news*, 29 April 2025

2 "IBM reportedly walks back diversity policies, citing 'inherent tensions': Here are all the companies rolling back DEI programs", Conor Murray and Molly Bohannon, *Forbes,* 11 April 2025

3 ibid.

4 ibid.

5 ibid.

6 Which companies are rolling back DEI policies?, Sam Forsdick, *Raconteur,* 29 May, 2025

7 "City body abandons diversity requirement as backlash grows", Matthew Field, *The Telegraph*, 30 January, 2025

8 "UK watchdogs scrap diversity and inclusion rules for financial firms", Martin Arnold, *Financial Times*, 12 March, 2025

9 "DEI is dead in America – now the City wants to kill it in Britain", Lucy Burton, *The Telegraph*, 6 February, 2025

10 "Brands – in this era of culture wars, don't give up on DEI&R", Bee Pahnke, *Campaign*, 11 December, 2024

11 ibid.

12 "Diversity is not a dirty word", Demi Abiola, *Campaign*, 14 January, 2025

13 "Has big business lost its mind or just its principles?", Tamryn Kerr, *Campaign,* 2025

14 "How can UK adland champion DE&I in the Donald Trump era?", Lucy Shelley, Campaign, 18 February, 2025

15 ibid.

16 ibid.

17 "As DEI enters its political football era, ad agency HR heads remain committed", Sam Anderson, *The Drum,* 20 January, 2025

18 "Accenture Song dropped from TfL creative review for 'not meeting DEI criteria'", Charlotte Rawlings, *Campaign*, 28 March, 2025

19 "It's not all bad in adland … five reasons to be cheerful right now", Tanya Whitehouse, *The Drum*, 23 April, 2025

20 "Woke vs anti-woke? Culture war divisions and

politics", *The Policy Institute,* Kings College London, October 2023

21 Nick Asbury, LinkedIn post, Jan 2025

22 "UK Supreme Court rules legal definition of a woman is based on biological sex", Ben Hatton, *BBC News,* 16 April, 2025

23 BBH | "This is undoubtedly a trans legal crisis... We need to ...Instagram · bbhlondon

24 "Gender policy in sport: What are the rules in football, cricket, boxing, netball and others after Supreme Court ruling?", *Sky Sports,* 3 May, 2025

25 "Where does the British public stand on transgender rights in 2024/25?", Matthew Smith, *YouGov,* 11 February, 2025

26 GD., LinkedIn post, 13 May, 2025

27 "Watch: More than 80 creative and media agencies join Global Climate Strike", Martha Llewellyn and Ben Londesbrough, *Campaign,* 20 September, 2019

28 "IPG, Apple and Budweiser among supporters of #blackouttuesday", Ben Londesbrough, *Campaign,* 2 June, 2020

29 "How can UK adland champion DE&I in the Donald Trump era?", Lucy Shelley

30 "I thought, 'Wow, I could probably do this': A Listers on their favourite TV ads of all time", Eszter Gurbitz, *Campaign,* 21 May, 2025

12: The barbarians at the gate

1 Shaping our Economy: senior roles in financial services and ... thebridgegroup.org.uk https://www.thebridgegroup.org.uk › progress-together

2 ibid.

3 Social Mobility Progression Report 2022: Mind the gap KPMG https://assets.kpmg.com › dam › pdf › 2022/12

4 Social class could be holding young people back from their ...KPMG https://kpmg.com › ... ›

5 "A Portrait of Modern Britain: Ethnicity and Religion", *Policy Exchange,* 14 October, 2024

6 Kevin Darton, Telephone conversation, 27 June, 2025

7 "INTERVIEW: Finza Aslam & Aaliyah Rice", Kevin Darton, *Pipeline,* 7 February, 2024

8 "Making the Creative Majority, All-Party Parliamentary Group for Creative Diversity", October 2023

9 "Young, diverse and in need of a break; how can the ad industry welcome talent from all walks of life?", Shanandore Robinson, *Shots,* 1 October, 2020

10 "Research highlights socio-economic barriers to advertising careers", Katie McQuater, *ResearchLive,* 25 January, 2023

11 ibid.

12 ibid.

13 ibid.

14 "Why Do Progressives Loathe the Working Class?", Alan Flanagan, *3am Thoughts*, 27 June, 2023

15 Paul Embery, *Despised: Why the Modern Left Loathes the Working Class*, Cambridge, 2021

16 "Survey reveals the exact demographics behind Reform's growing support", Paul Whitely, *Independent*, 5 June, 2025

17 "If you went to state school, do you ever feel British life is rigged against you? Welcome to the 93% Club", Alistair, Campbell, *The Guardian*, 19 June, 2025

18 David Goodhart, *The Road to Somewhere: The New Tribes Shaping British Politics*, London, 2017

19 "If you went to state school, do you ever feel British life is rigged against you? Welcome to the 93% Club", Alistair, Campbell

20 James Hillhouse, Telephone conversation, 29 July, 2025

21 ibid.

22 Undisclosed source, email exchange, 16 Sept, 2025

23 "I left the Tommy Robinson rally with the worrying realisation: this movement is only going to get bigger", Helen Pidd, *The Guardian*, 17 September, 2025

24 Ben Cobley, *The Tribe: The Liberal-Left and the System of Diversity*, Exeter, 2018

25 "Jonathan Haidt Discusses "De-Tot": Decentralized Totalitarianism", Eric Vieth, *Dangerous Intersections,* 6 August 2022

26 Steve Harrison, *Changing the World is the Only Fit Work for a Grown Man*, Gloucester, 2012

13: Or does the D stand for diversion?

1 "Madison Ave. blues: Why up to 70% of ad industry employees want to quit", *Forbes*, 7 October, 2015

2 "From 'sociopathic partners' to 'age discrimination': What's causing adland's morale problem?", *Campaign US*, 24 October, 2016

3 ibid.

4 "Everyone Disgusted With Ad Industry", Bob Hoffman, *The Ad Contrarian*, 24 October, 2016

5 "47% of ad industry employees report having low morale", David Kirkpatrick, *Marketing Dive*, 24 October, 2016

6 "Two-thirds of marketers have considered leaving

industry because of poor workplace wellbeing",
Rebecca Stewart, *The Drum*, 20 February, 2018

7 "Where DEI Went Wrong—And What Must Happen
   Next", Aparna Rae, *Forbes*, 12 March 2025; Jennifer
   C. Pan, *Selling Social Justice: Why the Rich Love
   Antiracism*, New York, 2025
8 "'A hard business': UK's illustrious ad industry tainted
   by burnout and inequality", Mark Sweney, *The
   Guardian,* 16 April, 2023
9 "The balance of power between agencies and staff has
   shifted", Sam Bradley, *The Drum*, 16 December, 2021
10 "Effective Employee Resource Groups are the Key to
   Inclusion at Work. Here's How to Get Them Right",
   Natacha Catalino, *McKinsey,* 7 December, 2022
11 Jennifer C. Pan, *Selling Social Justice: Why the Rich
   Love Antiracism*
12 ibid.; Frank Dobin and Alexander Kalev, *Getting to
   Diversity: What Works and What Doesn't*, Harvard,
   2022
13 Loris Vezzali and Sofia Stathi, Intergroup Contact
   Theory: Recent developments and future directions
   Current Issues in Social Psychology, London, 2016
14 Undisclosed source, email exchange, 1 August, 2025
15 Paul Burke, "Would Alan Parker have made it today",
   The Spectator, 4 August, 2020
16 Dave Dye, Email exchange, 1 September, 2025
17 "Nils Leonard: Uncommonly Creative", *Keith Smith*,
   Fuel Podcast, 23 April, 2022
18 "Everyone Disgusted With Ad Industry", Bob
   Hoffman
19 "Advertising giant WPP cuts diversity references from
   annual report", Simon Goodley, *The Guardian*, 30
   March, 2025
20 "Nearly half of adland employees could quit over

return-to-office mandates", Alessandra Scotto di Santolo, *Campaign*, 29 January, 2025

21 "An open letter to the gatekeepers of creative greatness", David Eakins, *Campaign*, 12 May, 2025

22 "Nabs helpline calls reach annual record of 5200", Alessandra Scotto di Santolo, *Campaign*, 12 February, 2025

23 "Facebook and Instagram owner Meta to enable AI ad creation by end of next year", Mark Sweney, *The Guardian*, 2 June, 2025

24 "'Change and fear' dominated at Cannes Lions as ad industry has less to roar about", Gideon Spanier, *Campaign*, 2 July, 2025

25 "This is meant to be fun. Why isn't this fun any more?", Josh Clarricoats, *The Drum,* 20 June, 2025

26 Undisclosed source, email exchange, 23 May, 2021

27 "This is meant to be fun. Why isn't this fun any more?", Josh Clarricoats

28 "ALL IN UK Advertising Census", *2025 Key Findings, Advertising Association, ISBA, IPA*

29 "All In Census 2025: results show some progress but participation falters", Eszter Gurbicz and Gideon Spanier, *Campaign*, 8 May 2025

30 "Employee Net Promoter Score (eNPS): The Ultimate 2025 Guide", Glen Siocan and Paula Garcia, AIHR

31 "All In Census reveals Adland's hybrid working stalemate", Nicola Kemp, *Creative Brief*, 8 May 2025

32 "Nils Leonard: Uncommonly Creative", *Keith Smith, Fuel Podcast*

Index

www.ingramcontent.com/pod-product-compliance
Lightning Source LLC
Chambersburg PA
CBHW031425270326
41930CB00007B/583

* 9 780957 151543 *